THE
CARD·PLAYER'S
OMNIBUS

Gyles Brandreth

Willow Books
Collins
8 Grafton Street, London W1X 3LA
1986

Other Collins Willow books you may enjoy:
The Monopoly Omnibus, Gyles Brandreth, 1985
The Rixi Markus Book of Bridge, Rixi Markus, 1985

Willow Books
William Collins Sons & Co Ltd
London · Glasgow · Sydney
Auckland · Toronto · Johannesburg

First published in Great Britain 1986
© Gyles Brandreth 1986

Designed by Clive Sutherland

British Library Cataloguing in Publication Data
Brandreth, Gyles
    The card player's omnibus
    1. Cards
    I. Title
    795.4   GV1243

ISBN 0-00-218235-1

Filmset by Rowland Phototypesetting Ltd,
Bury St Edmunds, Suffolk

Printed in Great Britain by
Hazell Watson & Viney Ltd, Aylesbury, Bucks

Contents

Introduction

Each of the main games dealt with in this book is set out with details of the number of players required, the cards used, the method of the deal, the objective of the game, how it is played and how it is scored. There are also hints on strategy, so that you can not only play each game, but play it well.

In order to avoid repetition, certain things are assumed to be the same for every game. Where there are variations from the norm, these will be made clear.

Here then are the general guidelines:

Number of players

Each player is assumed to be playing as an individual, unless it is stated that there are partnerships, in which case the partners sit opposite each other. It is conventional to refer to the four sides of the card table as North, South, East and West, with North partnering South, and East partnering West.

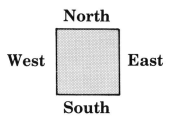

Cards

Where a normal pack is specified, this means a standard 52-card deck, with the cards ranked as follows: Ace (high), King, Queen, Jack, 10, 9, 8, 7, 6, 5, 4, 3, 2 (low).

The deal

The first dealer is determined by cutting the pack, with the player cutting the highest card becoming dealer. Thereafter the deal moves from player to player in a clockwise direction, starting with the player on the left of the dealer. Each card is dealt singly, unless specified in the text. Before each deal the pack is shuffled, and cut by the player to the dealer's right.

Objective

In some cases it is essential to know what one is aiming for in order to understand the game. In others, the objective becomes clear as the game is described.

In the first situation, a description of the objective is given before the play is described.

The bidding

In many games, a period of bidding takes place before the play starts. This

can be to determine a trump suit, or it can be a statement of intent to win a certain number of tricks. Indeed it can be a combination of both. The bidding always passes from player to player in a clockwise direction.

The play

A full description of how to play the cards is given for the first game in each section. For subsequent games, the reader may be referred back to the standard version.

The scoring

A full description is given of how to score each game, and how many points are required to win.

Strategy

For all the main games, and some of the variations, notes are included on the best tactics to employ. Often, the advice given for one game will be applicable to many.

Penalties for incorrect play have not been dealt with in great depth. I hope and trust that readers will abide by the rules of the game! If a crime is committed, I would suggest that the offender is punished by deducting from his or her score a certain number of points agreed beforehand by all the players.

A full Glossary of card player's jargon can be found on pp. 189 to 192.

Throughout the book I have referred to players as 'he'. This is not through chauvinism – it is merely in the interests of consistency and readability.

The History of Playing Cards

No one can be absolutely certain about the origin of playing cards.

One theory is that cards were invented in the Far East around 1120, in order to amuse the Emperor Seun Ho's concubines while they awaited their master's call.

A second theory maintains that they were invented in India by a Maharajah's wife, in order to wean him from his irritating habit of pulling on his beard.

Colourful though these explanations are, they do seem a little implausible. In fact it is likely that playing cards date much further back, to 800 or 900 A.D. The first cards were indeed found in the Far East, where they were initially used in religious ceremonies, and as paper money – although not only paper. Cards were made from thin strips of wood, ivory, metal, dried leaves and even tortoise shell.

It is interesting to compare the modern Chinese packs with our own present-day cards. Chinese cards are longer and thinner. And instead of spades, hearts, diamonds and clubs, the Chinese have Coins, Strings of Coins, Myriads of Strings of Coins, and Tens of Myriads of Strings of Coins. Imagine playing whist with Tens of Myriads of Strings of Coins as trumps!

9

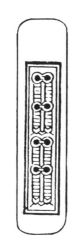

These Chinese cards are the three and eight in Coins, the three and eight in Strings of Coins, and the three and eight in Myriads of Strings of Coins.

Playing Cards in Europe

Cards reached Europe from the Far East early in the fourteenth century. They were brought by travellers, gypsies in caravans who liked playing cards because they were so portable and took up very little space.

The early European packs contained seventy-eight cards. There were four suits, each containing fourteen cards, and twenty-one tarot cards, used solely for the purposes of fortune telling. There was also a Joker, or Fool.

Gradually the single pack split into two, with the twenty-one tarot cards forming one pack, and the fifty-six playing cards another. The Joker suffered an identity crisis, and ended up going both ways. It stayed with the playing cards, where it was used in certain games, and also became integrated into the tarot pack.

The four suits originally represented four different classes of people.

There was the cup, representing the clergy; there was the sword, for the warriors; there was a coin, for the merchants, and there was a stave for the peasants.

In France these became hearts, spades, diamonds and clubs respectively, and Britain also adopted these names. Elsewhere in Europe, the suits remained nearer to their original identities.

10

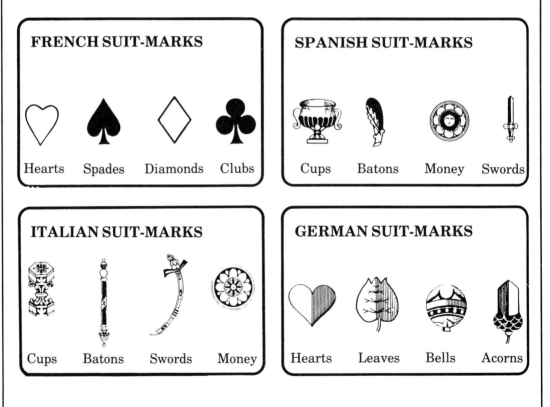

FRENCH SUIT-MARKS

Hearts   Spades   Diamonds   Clubs

SPANISH SUIT-MARKS

Cups   Batons   Money   Swords

ITALIAN SUIT-MARKS

Cups   Batons   Swords   Money

GERMAN SUIT-MARKS

Hearts   Leaves   Bells   Acorns

The fourteen cards in each suit consisted of numbers 1 to 10 and four court cards. These were, in descending order, the King, Queen, Knight and Jack.

The number was then reduced to thirteen. There were two reasons for this:

1 Thirteen was a very significant number in the Middle Ages, with strong links to the supernatural and the art of fortune-telling. There seemed a certain divine purpose in reducing the number of cards per suit to thirteen.
2 For the purposes of playing games, it was better to have an odd number of cards in each suit, because it increased the chances of a clear outcome.

Quite why the Knight was dropped is unclear. It was obvious that the King and Queen had to retain their status, but the decision to dispense with the services of the Knight rather than the Jack seems to have been arbitrary.

Having reduced each suit to thirteen cards, it was then decided that four court cards were needed after all. Rather than reinstating the Knight, the 1 was promoted above the King, and became the Ace. This rather confusing episode explains why the Ace is sometimes the highest card and sometimes the lowest card in contemporary card games.

Following these changes the French and British packs were in the state that we recognize today. In other parts of Europe, the packs were reduced still further.

In Spain, the 8, 9 and 10 were dropped, to form a 40-card pack. In Germany, the 2, 3, 4, 5 and 6 were dropped to form a 32-card pack. These reduced packs still live on in a number of modern-day games.

It may well be that the suit colours in our packs of cards also have a Far-Eastern origin. There is an ancient form of chess for four players, two players using red pieces and two using black, a remarkable parallel with our two red suits and two black suits.

It is curious to think that chess and cards may have a common ancestor. This theory is strengthened by the fact that there is another early form of chess in which pieces are placed on the board only when they are played, exactly like cards held in a hand.

Card playing can be bad for your health. In 1929 John and Myrtle Bennet were playing Bridge. Things were going badly, and were not helped when Myrtle criticized John's play. He slapped her, and in a fury she stormed from the room, fetched a gun and killed her husband with two well-aimed shots.

'Cards are war in disguise of sport.'

Charles Lamb

12

> **Significant Dates in the History of Playing Cards**
> **Eleventh century:**   the earliest surviving playing card dates back to this period. It was found in China, and is an honours card in the Coin suit.
> **1376:**   the first mention of playing cards in Europe, in a manuscript written in Latin by a German monk, Johannes, living in a Swiss monastery.
> **1392:**   the oldest surviving cards in Europe were manufactured. They belonged to King Charles VI of France, and are now exhibited in the Bibliothèque Nationale in Paris.
> **Early fifteenth century:**   the first mass-production cards were produced in Germany. They were engraved; previously all cards had been hand-painted.
> **1492:**   Christopher Columbus introduced cards to America, which is now the world's biggest market for playing cards. It is estimated that there are now 1 250 000 000 000 cards in the United States.

Playing cards have not always had an easy passage through the corridors of time. In the seventeenth century, at the height of Puritanism, cards were called 'The Devil's Picture Book' in Britain, because card-playing was thought to encourage idleness, gambling, and all sorts of other evils.

Nevertheless, rather like cigarettes these days, cards were considered by governments to be a necessary evil, and provided revenue in the form of card tax. This was first introduced to Britain in 1628, when it cost one farthing to own a pack of cards. Two hundred years later it had risen to half-a-crown, 12½p in modern currency. If the tax still existed today, and had kept pace with inflation, it would now cost several pounds to buy a pack of cards. Fortunately though it was abolished in 1828.

Politics and cards continued to mix, however, with political figures depicted on cards in the guise of royalty. In America, the early federalists disposed of the King of hearts, replacing him with a representation of George Washington, and renaming the card the President of hearts. The idea did not take off in a big way, but Washington is not the only president to have featured on the front of a playing card.

In the eighteenth and nineteenth centuries, some fascinating packs of cards were produced on which the ranks and suits of the cards were not explicitly shown, but were hidden within a subtle drawing. These were known as 'transformation packs'. They must have been a nightmare to play with, although they are a joy to look at.

Shown opposite are four cards from a pack which was first published in 1811. Can you identify them?*

* *7 clubs, 2 spades, 8 hearts, 10 diamonds.*

Note that one of the transformation cards depicts a soldier, the 'Triumphant Volunteer'. Cards have always had their role to play during wartime, with troops seeking cheap and portable entertainment between their sessions of combat duty. Some of the greatest games may first have been played in the trenches and bunker holes.

The number of different types of packs which have been produced over the past five centuries is astronomical. There have been political packs, transformation packs, educational packs, royal packs, packs for special occasions, celebrity packs, vulgar packs . . . the list is endless.

Understandably, many have become true collectors' items. An eighteenth-century pack of cards may fetch well over £1000 at auction. Even if you are not wealthy enough to become involved in this market, there are still hundreds of very affordable packs. And who knows, the cards which you buy in a local newsagent's today may be worth a fortune to your great-grandchildren!

The problem of playing cards out of doors in even a modest breeze was overcome by the invention of metal cards and a magnetic table.

In 1685 playing cards became the first paper currency of Canada, and the French Governor Jacques de Meulles paid off some war debts with them. During the French Revolution they were used as ration cards by Napoleon. In early America they were used as invitations to parties and balls and, when quartered, as visiting cards.

Early Games

The first card games to be played in Europe used the full 78-card pack, including the tarot cards. There were five suits: the four standard ones plus the tarots, which became known as triumphs, then finally trumps.

One of these games still survives in various parts of Europe. It is known as *Tarot* in France, *Tarock* in Austria and *Taroccho* in Italy.

As the tarots separated from the rest of the pack, new games emerged. The earliest which has direct descendants in the contemporary card world is the old Italian game of *Triomphe*. This spawned the French game of *Ecarté*, and it was Ecarté which was adopted in Britain – it is described later in this book.

Few of the early games are played now, although some have shown remarkable powers of survival. This is particularly true of *Piquet*, which is still extremely popular, and very widely played. The reason is quite simple – it is a great game.

The ancient Spanish game of *Ombre* is less frequently played, although it has a fine heritage, while *Primero*, the third of the early games we will examine, is virtually extinct.

Yet each is interesting in its own way. They are the forefathers of modern games, and it is obvious that many of their qualities have been passed down and utilized in the great card games we play today.

Piquet

Piquet is one of the oldest and finest card games. It originated in the fifteenth century, and was reputedly invented by Stephen de Vignoles, a chevalier of Charles VII. Since then it has always been well-favoured, although in recent years other two-player games such as Gin rummy have provided Piquet with stiff competition. Curiously, at no stage did Piquet ever catch on in the United States.

Number of players: Two.

Cards: A 32-card pack is used, with nothing lower than a 7. This particular pack is now best known as a 'piquet pack'. The cards have different values, eleven for an ace, ten for all court cards, and the face value for the other cards.

Objective: To score points for certain combinations of cards held, and for tricks taken.

The deal: Twelve cards are dealt to each player, in groups of two. The remaining eight form a stock pile.

Carte blanche: If either player is dealt a hand containing no court cards, he can declare carte blanche and claim ten points. The player declaring carte blanche must show his hand, but only after his opponent has exchanged (see below). This may mean reversing the normal order for exchange; if so, the non-dealer who has declared carte blanche must say how many cards he intends to exchange, so that the dealer can pick the remainder.

Exchange: The non-dealer exchanges first (except in the situation mentioned above). He can exchange anything from one to five cards. First he discards his unwanted cards, then draws the appropriate number from stock. If he does not draw his full quota of five, he can look at the other cards that he would have been entitled to. The dealer then exchanges in the same way, although the number of cards that are available to him will depend on the actions of the non-dealer. If there are still cards in stock after he has exchanged, he may look at them, although should he choose to do so the non-dealer has the same privilege.

Declarations: After the exchange come the declarations. There are three types of combination which are declared, although only the player with the higher-ranking combination scores points. The combinations are:

1   *Point* – the player with the most cards in a single suit scores one point for each card. If both players hold the same number of cards, the combination containing the higher total value wins, where the total value is the sum of the individual card values in the combination. e.g. If Player 1 has $\heartsuit$ A, Q, 10, 8, 7 and Player 2 has $\clubsuit$ K, J, 10, 8, 7, then Player 1's combination is worth (11 + 10 + 10 + 8 + 7) = 46, and Player 2's combination is worth (10 + 10 + 10 + 8 + 7) = 45, therefore Player 1 would score 5 points (one for each card in the combination).

2   *Sequence* – the player with the longest sequence of cards in a suit scores as follows:

three cards (*tierce*)	3 points
four cards (*quart*)	4 points
five cards (*quint*)	15 points

16

six cards (*sextet*)	16 points
seven cards (*septet*)	17 points
eight cards (*octet*)	18 points

If the two declared sequences are the same length, the sequence containing the highest card wins. If the two sequences are truly identical, no points are scored.

   The player with the winning sequence can also score for any other sequences held, but not previously declared.

3   **Set** – the player with the most cards of the same rank scores points as follows:

three cards (*trio*)	3 points
four cards (*quatorze*)	14 points

Only sets of cards above 9 can be counted. If two sets are the same length, the higher-ranking set wins. Thus four queens would beat four tens.

The process of declaration: This is designed to give away no more information than is necessary.

   For *point*, the non-dealer starts by saying 'Point of X', where X is the length of the point. If this is better than the dealer's point, the dealer says 'Good', and the non-dealer scores 1 for each card held in the combination. If it is worse, the dealer says 'Not good', and he scores 1 for each card held. If the points are equal, the dealer says 'How much?'. The non-dealer will tell the dealer the total value of the cards held in the combination, to which the dealer again replies 'Good' or 'Not good'. Again, one point is scored for each card in the combination. In rare cases the value as well as the length of the point will be equal. If so, no one scores.

   A similar series of statements follows for *sequence*, with the non-dealer announcing the length, and if necessary the highest card.

   For the *set*, the non-dealer announces whether he holds a trio or quatorze, and the value of the cards therein, for example, 'A trio of Kings'. The dealer simply says 'Good' or 'Not good', since there is no possibility of a tie.

   The winning combinations must always be shown to the loser.

The play: The non-dealer leads to the first trick, thereafter the winner of a trick leads to the next. A player must follow suit where possible, otherwise he discards any card. The highest card of the suit led wins the trick. There are no trumps.

Scoring for tricks: A player scores one point for winning a trick when he has led, two points for winning a trick when his opponent has led. If a player wins more than six tricks, he receives a bonus of ten points. If he wins all twelve, he receives a bonus of forty points, known as *capot*.

Additional scoring: There are two other ways in which points can be scored; these are for pique and repique.

Pique is scored by the non-dealer if he reaches thirty points before the dealer has scored anything. The reward for pique is thirty points.

Repique can be scored by either player if he scores thirty points on the declarations alone, without his opponent having scored anything. The reward for repique is sixty points.

Scoring for the game: A full game of piquet is normally played over six deals.

If at the end of six deals, both players have scored more than 100 points, the player with the higher score receives a bonus of 100 points plus the difference between his score and his opponent's.

If either or both players are under 100, the player with the higher score receives 100 points for winning plus the sum of his own and his opponent's scores.

For example, if the score at the end of six hands was Player A: 117 points, Player B: 108 points, then Player A would score 109 points: $(117 - 108) + 100$. If Player A had 126 points and Player B 94 points, Player A would score 320 points: $(126 + 94) + 100$.

Strategy: In Piquet you must concentrate on making points as non-dealer, for it is while you are non-dealer that you have the twin advantages of first exchange and opening lead.

It is *always* best to exchange five cards. By changing fewer, you are helping your opponent. The only situation in which you should change less than five cards is if it would seriously damage your potential combinations.

When you are dealer and exchanging second, think defensively. Try to retain a potential point suit, so as to avoid the possibility of pique, and keep good cards back to avoid the possibility of capot.

Finally, keep an eye on the score. If there is a high probability that you will fail to reach 100, try not to score any further points!

Ombre

For centuries Ombre was the national card game in Spain. It certainly dates back to the sixteenth century, and may be of even greater antiquity.

Nowadays it is very rarely played, which is odd really because it bears many of the hallmarks of contemporary card games – betting, bidding and trumping.

Perhaps it is the unusual ranking of cards which has tended to put people off. It certainly requires some effort to learn and remember it.

Number of players: Three.

Cards: A 40-card pack is used, with 8s, 9s and 10s stripped out.

Determining dealer: A new dealer is selected for each hand. This is done as follows: the previous dealer deals out cards until a black King appears. The player dealt the black King becomes the new dealer.

Betting: Each player must place one chip in a pot.

Objective: The successful bidder, who is known as 'ombre', must try to win more tricks than either of the other players.

The rankings of cards: This is where some people are put off – the rankings are unusual, and you'll need a good memory.

Before examining the ranking in non-trump suits, it is necessary to isolate some special trump cards.

The three highest trumps are called *matadors*. The first matador (*Spadille*) is always the Ace of spades, the third (*Basto*) is always the Ace of clubs. The second matador (*Manille*) is either a black 2 or a red 7 of the suit designated as trumps. If either red suit is trumps, the Ace of that suit becomes the fourth highest trump (*punto*), ranking immediately below the Ace of clubs.

For a suit which is not trumps, the cards are ranked as follows:

Red: King (high), Queen, Jack, Ace, 2, 3, 4, 5, 6, 7 (low).
Black: King (high), Queen, Jack, 7, 6, 5, 4, 3, 2 (low).

Where a black suit becomes trumps, the 2 of that suit is promoted and becomes the second matador.

Where a red suit becomes trumps, the 7 and Ace are promoted and become second matador and highest standard trump respectively.

To Summarize:

Top trumps

1	Spadille	Ace of spades
2	Manille	black 2 or red 7
3	Basto	Ace of clubs
4	Punto	red Ace (no punto if black)

Suit rankings

Red: K,Q,J,A*,2,3,4,5,6,7*
Black: K.Q.J.7.6.5.4.3.2*
* promoted when the suit is trumps.

The deal: Each player is dealt nine cards, in three groups of three. The remaining thirteen form a stockpile.

The bidding: Each player must, in turn, pass or offer to become ombre. If all pass, the cards are thrown in and another deal takes place, but with the old pot remaining.

If a player bids to become ombre, he can be overcalled by another player offering to play from hand (play his present set of cards, without exchanging only). A standard bid for ombre permits the player to exchange cards. The first bidder can overcall the second, if he is similarly prepared to play from hand.

The exchange: If ombre is not playing from hand, he can exchange any number of cards, taking replacements from stock, and placing the rejected cards on a discard pile. The second player can do likewise, and if there are any cards left, the same applies for the third. The old cards must be discarded before the new ones are drawn.

The play: Once the exchange has been completed, ombre announces the trump suit and leads to the first trick. A player must follow suit where possible, otherwise he can discard or play a trump card. The highest card played to a trick wins it, unless any trumps are played in which case the highest trump wins. The winner of a trick leads to the next.

The rules for play are slightly different for matadors. A low trump cannot force a player to play a matador, only another matador can. Thus if a low trump is led, and you hold no trumps other than matadors, it is perfectly legitimate to discard from another suit rather than play a matador.

Scoring: There are three possible outcomes to a hand:

1 *Sacardo* – ombre has taken more tricks than either opponent; he wins all the chips in the pot.
2 *Puesta* – at least one other player has tied with ombre; ombre must double the value of the pot.
3 *Codille* – one of ombre's opponents has taken more tricks than ombre; ombre must pay the value of the pot to the opponent who has taken the majority of tricks.

In the case of puesta or codille, the value of the pot is carried forward to the next hand.

Strategy: The most important thing in Ombre is simply to remember the rankings, and to be able to assess the strength of your hand accordingly. In view of the exchange, a hand containing two good suits is usually very promising as you may well be able to strengthen them through the exchange.

Unlike Piquet, it is not usually best policy to exchange a lot of cards – this tends to indicate a weak hand. Just discard the worthless cards, rather than fishing hopefully for good ones.

Finally, when another player is ombre, remember that the main objective must be to prevent him making sacardo. This may mean sacrificing tricks that you could win in order that the other defender can take the trick. It is far better for one defender to win every trick than to divide them evenly.

Primero

The history of royalty and playing cards seems irrevocably intertwined. The cards reflect the royalty, with their array of court cards, while the real kings and queens have always played a leading role in the spread of card games.

This was the case even back in the sixteenth century, when both King Henry VIII and Queen Elizabeth I of England were keen players of the gambling game Primero.

Cardano, the great sixteenth-century mathematician, described Primero as 'noblest of them all'. Few would agree today, but it is of interest to look at the game and to see how many of its features have been retained in current favourites such as poker.

Number of players: Two to ten.

Cards: A 40-card pack is used, with 8s, 9s and 10s stripped out. The cards are valued as follows:

> 2 = twelve points; 3 = thirteen points; 4 = fourteen points; 5 = fifteen points; 6 = sixteen points; Ace = sixteen points; 7 = twenty-one points; all court cards = ten points.

The deal: Each player is dealt four cards.

Betting: Players place bets according to the quality of their hands.

The show: Once all the bets have been placed, the players show their hands. The highest hand wins the pot. The hands are ranked as follows:

1 *Chorus* – four cards of the same rank.
2 *Fluxus* – four cards of the same suit (a flush).
3 *Supremus* – Ace–6–7 in any suit.
4 *Primero* – one card in each suit.
5 *Numerus* – a two- or three-card flush.

If two cards are equally ranked, the winning hand is one with the higher point count, based on the card values.

21

According to Shakespeare, King Henry VIII spent the night Jane Seymour gave birth to his son Edward playing Primero.

The Euchre Family

Euchre is the main representative in a large family of five-card trick and trump games.

It may be that the Euchre family shares, with the Whist family, a common ancestor in the ancient Spanish game of Triumph. Certainly it appears to have reached North America, where it really took hold in the 1860s, via Europe.

As more sophisticated games were developed in the twentieth century, Euchre became less popular, although it is still widely played in the north-west states of America and, curiously, in the West Country in Britain.

Like all great card games, it is simple at heart, but with many hidden depths. There are numerous versions, for varying numbers of players, but undoubtedly the classic form of Euchre is the four-player partnership game.

Partnership Euchre

Number of players: Four, forming two partnerships.

Cards: The 32-card piquet pack is used, with all cards below the 7 stripped out. Ace is high, with other cards ranked, in descending order, K, Q, J, 10, 9, 8, 7. The highest card in the chosen trump suit is the Jack (known as *right bower*). The second highest trump (known as *left bower*) is the Jack of the other suit the same colour as the trump suit. For example, if hearts were trumps, the full order of the trump suit would be JH (highest), JD, AH, KH, QH, 10H, 9H, 8H, 7H (lowest).

The deal: Five cards are dealt to each player, in groups of three, then two. The top card from the remainder of the pack is then turned up, to set the prospective trump suit.

Determining trumps: Starting with the player to the left of the dealer, each in turn has the opportunity to accept the prospective trump suit. Acceptance represents a commitment to make at least three of the five tricks, with or without help from his partner.

The opponents of the dealer signify acceptance by saying 'I order it up.' The dealer's partner accepts by saying 'I assist.' Following either of these actions, the dealer tacitly agrees the call by picking up the exposed card, at the same time discarding a card from his hand.

The dealer can still accept the trump suit even if the others have all passed. He signifies his intention by saying 'I take it up.' If all refuse, a second round of bidding follows in which players can nominate their own trump suit, again starting with the left-hand opponent.

If all pass a second time, the hand is abandoned and the deal passes on to the left.

As soon as any player has made an acceptance bid, the bidding ends and play begins.

The successful bidder has the option of playing alone. If the bidder requests this, his partner must place his hand face-down on the table and take no further part in the hand. The bidder must attempt to make sufficient tricks unassisted.

The play: The opening lead is made by the player to the left of the dealer, except where someone is playing alone, in which case the opening lead is made by the player to his left. Each player contributes one card to each trick.

A player must follow suit if he is able to. If a player cannot follow suit, he can either discard or play a card from the trump suit. The left bower is treated just like any other trump card. If its own suit is led, there is no obligation to play it.

The highest card played to a trick wins it, unless any trumps have been played, in which case the highest trump wins. The winner of a trick leads to the next.

The hand ends when all the cards have been played.

The scoring: If the bidding side wins all five tricks, known as *winning the march*, it scores two points. If the successful bidder has played alone and won the march, his side scores four points.

If the bidding side makes three or four tricks, it receives one point, regardless of whether the hand was played alone or in partnership.

If the bidding side makes only one or two tricks, the opposition is awarded two points.

A game is generally played up to five points. Traditionally, scoring is done using the discarded cards, rather than on paper. The following diagram shows the methods of scoring one, two, three and four points:

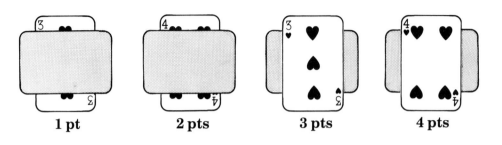

| 1 pt | 2 pts | 3 pts | 4 pts |

Strategy: The first and third players must bear in mind that the dealer will be picking up the exposed card, should they decide to bid. At least two trumps including a bower, plus one outside winner, would be the minimum requirements for a sensible bid. The second player is in a stronger position, and would probably bid on any two trumps and one trick outside. The dealer, should the bidding pass round to him, will usually accept the trump suit, unless he is extremely weak. By passing, he would allow the first player to nominate any suit as trumps, perhaps setting up a march.

Much, of course, depends on the state of the score. At 1–4 down, it might be worth 'going alone' if a strong hand is held, whereas at 4–1 up, the same hand could be played in partnership.

When playing a hand, it is often best to draw trumps, thus setting up other cards as potential winners. It is always worth remembering that only 20 of the 32 cards are actually in play. Thus if you have a King on its own, there is a very good chance that it will win even though the Ace is out somewhere.

Sample Hands – Partnership Euchre
There are four players, Nigel and Sue forming one partnership (N and S), William and Emma the other (W and E).

Several hands have already been played, and as Sue prepares to deal she checks the score to find that she and Nigel are 2–3 down. The cards are dealt as follows:

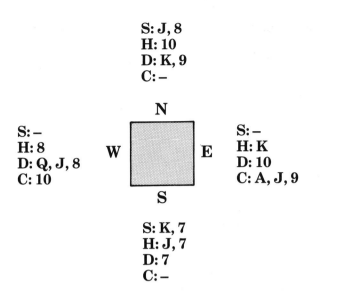

S: J, 8
H: 10
D: K, 9
C: –

N

S: –
H: 8
D: Q, J, 8
C: 10

W

E

S: –
H: K
D: 10
C: A, J, 9

S

S: K, 7
H: J, 7
D: 7
C: –

7C is turned up.

William must pass. If the bidding entered a second round he would nominate diamonds as trumps, hoping to make three tricks in that suit.

Nigel also passes. He has the left bower (JS), but very little else.

Emma has a much stronger hand. Her hand certainly looks good for three tricks, and there is the chance of a march if William has a strong card in diamonds. She says 'I order it up', and Sue then takes 7C, discarding 7D face-down.

Trick 1:   Emma's bid is obviously based on strong clubs, so William decides to lead 10C. Nigel plays JS, as he must. Emma plays JC and Sue plays 7C.

Trick 2:   Emma decides to clear out any more trumps. She leads AC. Sue discards 7H, William discards 8H, Nigel discards 8S.

Trick 3:   Emma decides that now is the time to test out the diamonds, just in case she places William in the awkward position of having to choose a discard with, say, two Kings in separate suits. She leads 10D. Sue discards JH. William plays QD. Nigel wins with KD. So much for the march!

Tricks 4 and 5:   Nigel leads 9D, which Emma trumps with 9C. Her KH now wins the fifth trick, the other players' discards being irrelevant.

William and Emma have won four tricks, giving them one point and taking the overall score to 4–2.

The deal now transfers to William, and the cards come out as follows:

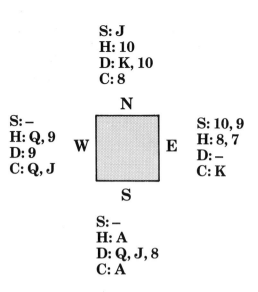

S: J
H: 10
D: K, 10
C: 8

S: –
H: Q, 9
D: 9
C: Q, J

S: 10, 9
H: 8, 7
D: –
C: K

S: –
H: A
D: Q, J, 8
C: A

KS is turned up.

Nigel starts the bidding. He has the right bower, but there is little else to recommend the hand. He passes. Emma also passes. Sue has a beautiful hand – but not with spades as trumps! She passes, hoping that she will have the chance of going alone in a second round of bidding, nominating diamonds as trumps.

William must make a decision. He decides to accept trumps; he has the left bower, and coupled with the King this should hopefully bring in two tricks. If Emma can contribute one trick, they may scrape home. 'I'll take it up' he announces, and discards 9D.

Trick 1: Nigel has the opening lead. He has no obvious card, but eventually decides on 8C. Emma plays KC, Sue plays the Ace and William the Queen.

Trick 2: Sue plays AH, the other three following with 9H, 10H and 7H.

Trick 3: Sue now leads QD. William trumps with KS. Nigel plays 10D and Emma discards 8H.

Trick 4: William now leads JC, fingers crossed. But it is not to be. Nigel triumphantly places JS on it, giving his partnership a third trick.

Trick 5: Emma's final trump wins, but it is too late.

Nigel and Sue score two points for breaking the contract, making the score 4–4, and setting things up for a very exciting hand which will determine the outcome of the game.

But take a closer look at the cards for the last hand. If William had not 'taken it up', Sue would have played alone in diamonds, and had absolutely no trouble making all five tricks, winning the game in the process. So William in fact made a very worthwhile sacrifice.

Partnership euchre can easily be adapted as a two- or three-player game. In **Three-handed euchre**, the caller always plays on his own, and scores three points for winning a march. In **Two-handed euchre**, the pack is reduced to 24 cards by discarding the 7s and 8s, with the march again scoring three points.

Ecarté

Ecarté is a very old French game, first played in the early 1800s, and prevalent in French casinos right up to the 1970s. The word 'écarté' means 'discarded'.

Number of players: Two.

Cards: The 32-card piquet pack is used, with all cards below 7 stripped out. The ranking of cards is slightly unusual: K (high), Q, J, A, 10, 9, 8, 7 (low). Note the position of the Ace.

The deal: Each player is dealt five cards, in groups of three, then two. The top card from the remainder of the pack is turned up and sets the trump suit.

Exchanging cards: If the non-dealer is unhappy with his hand, he says 'Cards,' proposing to exchange any number of them for cards from stock. If the dealer accepts the proposal, he then deals as many cards as the non-dealer requests, taking the same number back and placing them aside. The dealer can then exchange the same number of his own cards.

This process can be repeated, although at any stage the dealer can refuse the proposal, thus ending the exchange.

The non-dealer indicates his acceptance of his hand, before or during card-exchange, by making the opening lead.

The play: Following the non-dealer's lead, play proceeds as in Euchre (page 22), except for two slight differences:

1   If a player can win a trick, he *must* do so.
2   If a player cannot follow suit, and can trump, he must do so. He cannot discard.

The scoring: One point is scored for making three or four tricks. Two points are scored for making all five (known as *the vole*). If either player has refused to exchange, and fails to make three tricks, his opponent receives one point. If either player holds the King of trumps, he receives one point *provided it is declared before play starts*. Game is five points.

Thackeray was a great admirer of the game Ecarté, so much so that it appears in two of his works, *Vanity Fair* and *Barry Lyndon*.

Napoleon

Often referred to simply as Nap, this game is similar to Euchre, but with everyone playing as individuals.

Number of players: Two to eight.

Cards: One normal pack is used.

The deal: Five cards are dealt to each player.

The bidding: Starting with the player to the left of the dealer, each player in turn has the opportunity to bid or pass, with each bid being higher than the previous one. The level of the bid indicates the number of tricks the player proposes to make, with his chosen suit as trumps. The suit is not actually mentioned during the bidding. The lowest bid is two, followed by three, four and five (known as *Napoleon*). There is one other bid, higher than Napoleon. This is *Wellington* – it also proposes winning five tricks, but with the scores for success, or the penalties for failure, doubled. Wellington can only appear if Napoleon has; in other words, a bid of four cannot be followed by a bid of Wellington.

There is only one round of bidding.

The play: The successful bidder leads. The suit led is trumps. Thereafter the play is the same as in Euchre.

The scoring: The rewards for success and the penalties for failure are normally paid in chips, although scores can be kept on paper. They are as follows:

	Success	Failure
Bid of two	2	2
Bid of three	3	3
Bid of four	4	4
Napoleon	10	5
Wellington	20	10

If the bidder is successful, he is paid the amount by each of the other players. If he fails, he pays them.

Strategy: Napoleon is not a complicated game, and the skill lies mainly in being able to judge the strength of your hand, and its trick-taking capabilities. Having the opening lead, and thus being able to drive out other players' trumps, is very important. It can make a weak hand with a long suit worth bidding on.

A popular variation on straight Nap is to include a bid of *misere* which ranks between three and four. It is a declaration to lose every trick, with no trump suit. The stakes paid are the same as for a bid of three.

It is also possible to add a bid of *Blücher*, which ranks above Wellington, and trebles the rewards and penalties associated with a bid of Napoleon.

One of the more interesting variations is **Purchase Nap**, in which an unlucky player is allowed to buy his way out of trouble. He can exchange any number of his cards for those in stock, but must pay one chip into a pot for each card he exchanges. The pot is accumulated until any player achieves a bid of Napoleon (or higher), in which case he wins the total contents of the pot.

In **Widow Nap**, or **Sir Garnet**, an extra hand of five cards is dealt. Any player, in his turn, may pick up this hand and add it to their own, then discard five unwanted cards. There is just one snag: picking up the *widow*, as the extra hand is called, commits the player to a bid of Napoleon. Not only that; if he fails to fulfil the bid, his penalty is doubled up to ten chips, although the reward for success does not change.

♥ ♣ ♦ ♠

Skat

Skat is the German national card game. It is not easy to learn, but rewards the card connoisseur who is prepared to master it. It is played world-wide, and is undoubtedly the finest three-player card game. In Germany itself, Skat is a national institution. Half the population knows how to play, and millions tune in to the country's televised Skat championships.

Number of players: Three.

Cards: The 32-card piquet pack is used, with all cards below 7 stripped out. The ranking of cards varies according to the denomination of the contract:

1 ***A trump contract*** (e.g. hearts as trumps)
   Trumps   JC (high), JS, JH, JD, AH, 10H, KH, QH, 9H, 8H, 7H (low).
   Other suits   A (high), 10, K, Q, 9, 8, 7 (low).

2 ***A grand contract*** (a special form of trump contract)
   Trumps   JC (high), JS, JH, JD (low).
   All suits   A (high), 10, K, Q, 9, 8, 7 (low).

3 ***A no-trump contract***
   All suits   A (high), K, Q, J, 10, 9, 8, 7 (low).

31

Cards also have point values, regardless of the contract. They are as follows:

Ace	11 points
10	10 points
King	4 points
Queen	3 points
Jack	2 points

The total value of the pack is 120 points.

Objective: All players attempt to win the right to choose the game to be played; the successful bidder, the declarer, then tries to make the number of game points required to fulfil his bid.

The deal: Ten cards are dealt to each player, in groups of three, four and three. The remaining two, which are put aside after the first round of dealing, are known as the *skat*.

Designation of players: The player to the dealer's left is called *forehand*, the second player is *middlehand*, and the dealer himself is known as *endhand*.

Hand evaluation: Before looking at the bidding, it is necessary to have an understanding of hand evaluation; the maximum bid any particular hand justifies, based on its prospective game value.

   There are two types of play available to the declarer; trick-taking and misere.

Evaluation of trick-taking hands

The first and most important point is that failure to capture over half the card points represents immediate defeat. This means at least 61 points are required, in tricks taken plus (voluntarily) the skat. If the target is achieved, it is known as 'making the game'.

So, assuming there is a reasonable chance of making the game, the hand's prospective game value can be calculated. This is the base value of the proposed trump suit, multiplied by the total number of scoring factors.

The base values are as follows:

Diamonds	9 points
Hearts	10 points
Spades	11 points
Clubs	12 points
Grand	20 points

There are seven main scoring factors:

1 *Game* – automatic scoring factor of one for making the game.
2 *Playing from hand* – if the declarer chooses to play without looking at the skat, this acts as a scoring factor of one.
3 *Matadors* – the Jack of clubs and all trumps in unbroken sequence beneath it are known as matadors. Each matador constitutes a scoring factor of one. For example, if a player holds JC, JS and JH, this represents a scoring factor of three.

   Just as the possession of matadors produces a scoring factor, so too does the lack of them. If a hand does not have JC and JS, but does hold JH, it is said to be 'without two matadors' – this represents a scoring factor of two.
4 *Schneider* – 90+ card points won by declarer; scoring factor of one.
5 *Schwartz* – all ten tricks taken; scoring factor of two.
6 *Schneider predicted* – 90+ points won by declarer, the intention of which was announced before play started; scoring factor of three.
7 *Schwartz predicted* – all ten tricks taken, the intention of which was announced before play started; scoring factor of four.

Schneider predicted or schwartz predicted must be done without the skat.

An example may clarify the situation. Consider the following hand:

Spades	J, K
Hearts	A, 10, Q, 8
Diamonds	10, 7
Clubs	J, 8

This hand contains two matadors, and a very strong heart suit. It looks certain to make game, and there is a chance of Schneider if there are good cards in the skat. So, based on a total scoring factor of at least three, probably four, the hand looks good for a bid up to 40. If successful, hearts would obviously be named as trumps.

Evaluation of misere hands

Here the intention is to lose every trick. There are four misere bids, each with a distinct value:

23   misere played after exchanging through the skat.
35   misere played only from the hand dealt.
46   misere played with the hand exposed, but after exchanging through the skat.
59   misere played open, and with the hand dealt.

The bidding: Middlehand starts by bidding or passing. The bid is simply a number; the actual game is announced only when the bidding has finished.

If middlehand bids, then forehand replies, either by passing, or by saying 'Hold'. If he holds, then middlehand must raise his bid or pass.

As soon as either passes, endhand can enter the bidding, taking the role of forehand. In other words, he can either pass, or match the previous player's bid by saying 'Hold'.

If both middlehand and forehand pass originally, endhand may make a bid. A player who has passed cannot then enter the bidding.

Once two players drop out, the remaining bidder becomes the declarer.

The skat: The declarer can look at the skat, and decide whether or not to use the cards in it. If he chooses to, he discards two of his own. If he decides to play from hand, ignoring the skat, one point is added to the scoring factor total.

The games: The declarer must now announce the game for the hand. If he has taken from the skat, he is restricted to choosing a trump suit, grand, misere or open misere. If he has decided to play from hand, he can also announce his intention of going for schneider or schwartz. The scoring factor is incremented according to the game. Matadors, however, do not have to be announced until the end of the hand.

The play: Forehand always leads, regardless of who is declarer. The play is the same as in *Euchre* (page 22), with players following suit where possible, trumping or discarding if unable to follow.

The hand ends when all cards have been played.

The scoring: If declarer has chosen a suit or grand as trumps, he adds up the card points in tricks taken, and adds these to the value of the two cards in the skat. This gives his total trick points. In a misere contract, the skat is discarded.

If the total is greater than 61, he has made the game. Next he must see whether he has made the bid.

In a misere hand, providing the declarer's bid was not greater than the misere value, and provided he has made no tricks, he has won.

In any other game, the final value of the hand must be calculated, with the final total of scoring factors and the base value of trumps being multiplied together. Provided this is not less than the declarer's bid, then he has won.

However, if declarer predicted schneider or schwartz, and failed, then he has lost even if he succeeded in making game.

Only the declarer scores (or loses) points on a hand. If he has succeeded, he scores the game value, which will normally be higher than his bid. If he has succeeded in misere, he receives the misere value.

If the declarer has failed, either through failing to make game, his bid, a predicted schneider or schwartz, or an attempted misere, then the game value he would have scored had he succeeded is deducted from his score.

Skat is usually played for small stakes, over a period of time. An average score is worked out, with players above the average being paid by those below.

Strategy: Skat is not a simple game, and elements such as hand evaluation come only with experience. Nevertheless, there are some things which can be kept in mind and should make decisions a little easier.

Always be aware of the number of trumps. Eleven out of the thirty cards in play are trumps in a suit contract. This means that potential winners will often be trumped; if you have a long suit with strong cards in it, draw out the trumps first.

Remember that there are four trumps higher than the Ace. If you are the declarer and hold the Ace, guard it carefully.

When opposing a declarer, throw high-value cards on your defensive partner's winners. Don't let the declarer pull in the card points.

Above all, remember the unusual ranking of the cards. Good luck!

Five Hundred

So named because five hundred is the points target for victory, this is a close relative of the Whist family's most famous offspring, Bridge. Unlike most card games, Five hundred did not develop naturally from other, similar games. It was invented and copyrighted by the American Playing Card Company in 1904, in an attempt to provide a game 'intermediate in difficulty between Euchre and Whist'. It succeeded admirably.

Number of players: Three.

Cards: The 32-card piquet pack is used, but with a Joker added, making a total of 33 cards.

In a trump contract, the Joker ranks highest above the right and left bowers (see *Euchre* page 22).

In a no-trump contract, the Joker ranks above the Ace, and can be placed in any suit its holder desires.

The deal: Ten cards are dealt to each player, in groups of three, two, three and two. The remaining three cards are placed face-down on the table, to form a 'widow', an extra hand which comes into play at a later stage.

The bidding: Starting with the player on the dealer's left, each player has the opportunity to bid or pass. If a player passes, he is excluded from any further bidding.

A bid signifies the number of tricks the bidder proposes to make, and the trump suit. The suits are ranked as follows: no trumps (highest), hearts, diamonds, clubs, spades (lowest). The lowest bid is six, the highest ten. Therefore the bids range from Six Spades (lowest) to Ten No Trumps (highest). Each bid must be higher than the previous one. The bidding ends when two successive players pass, in which case the last bid becomes the contract.

The successful bidder has the right to add the three cards in the widow to his own hand, discarding the three least useful cards. This should enter consideration during the bidding.

If everyone passes on the first round, the hand is abandoned and the deal passes to the next player.

The play: This is identical to the play in *Partnership euchre* (page 23), except that the successful bidder always leads to the first trick.

If the Joker is led in a no-trump contract, the player leading it must specify which suit it represents, and the others must follow suit. It cannot represent a suit on which its holder has already discarded.

When he is not on lead, the holder of the Joker in a no-trump contract can only play it if he has no cards in the suit led.

It must always win the trick on which it is played.

The hand ends when all cards have been played.

The scoring: The successful bidder is awarded points according to the number of tricks he has contracted to make, and the trump suit chosen. No points are awarded for overtricks, unless all ten tricks are made, in which case if the value of the contract is less than 250, the player is awarded exactly 250 points. The table of contracts is as follows:

Tricks bid	S	C	D	H	No trumps
6	40	60	80	100	120
7	140	160	180	200	220
8	240	260	280	300	320
9	340	360	380	400	420
10	440	460	480	500	520

The opponents of a contract are awarded ten points for every trick they take between them.

If the successful bidder fails to make his contract, its value is deducted from his score.

For example, if Player 1 bid Seven Diamonds, and made eight tricks, he would score 180 points, and his opponents would score 20 points each. If he made only six tricks, he would have 180 deducted from his score, and his opponents would score 40 each.

Three-Card Loo

Also known as **Lanterloo**, this was once Europe's most widely played card game. It is a gambling game and, like Poker, there is no pleasure in Loo without stakes.

Number of players: Three to sixteen.

Cards: One normal pack is used.

The deal: Three cards are dealt to each player and an additional hand, known as the 'miss', is dealt and placed next to the dealer. The top card from the remainder of the pack is turned up to set trumps.

Stakes: Each player must place three chips in a pot before play commences.

The choice: Starting with the player on the dealer's left, each player has three choices:

1   To play with the cards dealt to them ('I play').
2   To exchange their cards for the miss, and play with it instead ('I take the miss').
3   To pass, taking no further part in the hand.

If everyone passes, the dealer takes the pot. If only one player has stayed in and has not taken the miss, the dealer must play him using the miss – although the dealer in this situation does not pay or get paid. If one player remains and has taken the miss, the dealer has the choice of playing for normal stakes, or dropping out and allowing the player to take the pot.

The play: The first player to the dealer's left who has chosen to stay in leads to the first trick, and must play his highest trump if he has one. All players then follow. They *must* attempt to win the trick. In other words, each player must, if possible, play a higher card then the highest already played, or a higher trump if they cannot follow suit.

The winner of a trick takes one-third of the pot. He must then lead his highest trump, if he has any.

Looing: Any player who has participated in a hand, but failed to win a trick, is said to have been 'looed', and must pay an extra three chips into the next pot.

A player is also looed if he plays out of turn, fails to attempt to take a trick, or fails to lead his highest trump.

One popular variation is for a trump flush – three cards in the trump suit – automatically to win the pot.

Five-card loo

In Five-card loo each player is dealt five cards instead of three, and must contribute five chips to the pot. No miss is dealt.

Exchange: Each player can exchange any number of cards, taking their replacements from the top of stock. Having exchanged, a player cannot then drop out of the hand.

Pam: The Jack of clubs, known as *pam*, is the highest trump, regardless of which suit is trumps.

Flushes and blazes: Before play commences, a player holding five cards in the same suit, or four cards plus pam, can expose his hand and claim the pot. This is a *flush*. If there is more than one flush, the rules are as follows:

1 A trump flush beats a plain flush.
2 For two plain flushes, the hand containing the higher card wins.

A *blaze* is a hand made up entirely of court cards. This also takes the pot, and beats any flush.

The play: This is identical to *Three-card loo* (page 37), and the same rules apply concerning looing; but with the fine increased to five chips.

♥ ♣ ♦ ♠

The All-Fours Family

The ancient game of All-fours was first played over three hundred years ago in Kent. Nowadays it is virtually extinct in Britain, and it has never been played elsewhere in Europe. However, although it failed to cross the channel, All-fours did bridge the Atlantic, and it is now more popular in America than anywhere else in the world.

The name 'All-fours' derives from the four key scoring elements in the game, details of which are described overleaf.

Seven-Up

Seven-up, so named because seven points are required to win, is the most widely played of the original All-fours games. It is also known as High-low-Jack and Old sledge.

Number of players: Two or three.

Cards: Normal pack.

The deal: Each player is dealt six cards, three at a time. The next card is turned up and placed on the remainder of the pack, which acts as a stock pile. If the card turned up is a Jack, the dealer is awarded one point.

Determining trumps: The player to the dealer's left can either *stand* or *beg*. If he stands, this means that he agrees that the card turned up will designate the trump suit. By begging, he passes the decision to the dealer. If the dealer is happy with the proposed trump suit, a point is awarded to the 'begger', then play commences. Otherwise, three further cards are dealt to each player and a second card is turned face up. If this card is of a different suit from the first, then this new suit becomes trumps. If it is of the same suit, three more cards are dealt, with the process being repeated until a new suit does appear. If at any stage a Jack is turned up, the dealer receives one point. If the pack is exhausted before a trump suit has been set, the whole hand must be redealt.

The play: Once trumps have been established, each player must reduce his hand, if necessary, to six cards. This is done by discarding superfluous ones face down. The player to the dealer's left leads. If a player cannot follow suit, he can either trump or discard. The hand ends when all cards have been played.

The scoring: A maximum of four points is available on any one hand. They are scored as follows:

1   *High* – a point is awarded to the player dealt the highest trump.
2   *Low* – a point is awarded to the player dealt the lowest trump.
3   *Jack* – a point is awarded either to the dealer, if the Jack is turned up, or to the player who wins the trick containing the Jack of trumps. If the Jack of trumps has not appeared, the point for Jack is not awarded.
4   *Game* – a point is awarded to the player scoring the highest card-point value in tricks taken, where the Ace scores four points, the King three, the Queen two, the Jack one and the 10, appropriately enough, ten points. If two players tie, the Game point is not awarded.

The first player to reach seven points wins the game.

Strategy: Obviously there is no skill attached to being dealt a particular card. What skill there is lies in the play of the cards. It is important to guard one's 10s, as they usually determine the destination of the Game point.

There is also a certain amount of strategy in the determination of trumps. If a player needs only one point for victory, he will be happy to have as trumps any suit in which he holds the Ace or King, regardless of whether he has any other cards in the suit.

Under normal circumstances, one would not feel comfortable about the trump suit unless three of the suit were held, or two including the Ace or King.

Sample Hand – Seven-Up

There are three players, Alan, Ben and Carrie, henceforth referred to as A, B and C.

Alan deals the cards as follows:

	A	B	C
Spades	A, Q, 4	2	7
Hearts	6	A, 4	10, 9, 3
Diamonds	–	5, 3	Q, J
Clubs	7, 3	10	–

8S is turned up from stock.

Ben chooses to beg, but secretly hopes that Alan will accept spades as trumps, so that he will receive a point immediately, with the guarantee of another for the low trump.

Alan does.

Trick 1: B leads AH, C plays 3H, A plays 6H. Already it is clear that Carrie's chances of winning a trick containing her 10H are slight.

Trick 2: B leads 4H, C plays 10H, A trumps with 4S – ten points for Alan!

Trick 3: A leads AS, B plays 2S, C plays 7S.

Trick 4: A leads QS, B discards 3D, C discards 9H.

Trick 5: A leads 3C, B plays 10C, C discards JD.

Trick 6: B leads 5D, C plays QD, A discards 7C. At last a trick for Carrie, but little more than consolation value.

The scoring: Alan has the following cards in tricks taken – 10H, AS and QS, worth 10, 4 and 2 card-points, total 16.

Ben has taken AH, 10C and JD – 4, 10 and 1 respectively, total 15.

Carrie has only QD, total 2.

Thus the point for Game goes to Alan, as does the point for High. The point for Low goes to Ben. There is no point for Jack.

It is easy to see why All-fours in its original form is rarely played these days. It is somewhat laborious and relies more on luck than skill.

Attempts to strike a better balance include a variation whereby the point for Low is awarded not to the player dealt the lowest trump, but to the player winning the trick containing it.

A four-person version developed, with players in partnership, rather than playing as individuals.

Further innovations involved the scoring system. In **All fives**, the play is identical to Seven-up, but additional points are awarded to the players capturing tricks containing certain trump cards as follows:

Ace	4 points
King	3 points
Queen	2 points
Jack	1 point
Ten	10 points
Five	5 points

Thus a trick containing AH, KH, 8H and 5H, where hearts are trumps, would score 4 + 3 + 5 = 12 points. Generally a game of All-fives is played up to 61 points.

As is the case with many groups of card games, there is a member of the All-fours family which involves drawing cards from a stock pile.

California Jack

This game is alternatively known as **California loo** or the more descriptive **Draw seven-up**.

Number of players: Two.

Cards: Normal pack.

The deal: Six cards are dealt to each player. The remainder of the pack forms a stock pile, of which the top card is turned up and designates the trump suit for the first trick.

The play: As each trick is played, the two players replenish their hands from the stock pile, and the next card is turned up to reset the trump suit. Once the stock is exhausted, the players play out their remaining cards with the last trump suit being used.

The scoring: One point is scored for each of the following cards contained in tricks won: the lowest trump, the highest trump and the Jack of trumps. In addition there is a point for Game, exactly as in *Seven-up* (page 40).

California Jack can also be played with three or four players. With three, one of the four 2s must be discarded. With four the full pack is used. In both cases, all players draw after each trick.

Shasta Sam is played in exactly the same way as California Jack, except that the trumps are established by cutting the pack, and remain for the whole deal. The cards drawn from the stock pile remain face-down throughout, so that the winner of the previous trick does not know which card he will draw.

Auction Pitch

Known also as **Setback**, Auction pitch is now the most popular member of the All-fours family, and is very widely played in the United States.

Number of players: Two to seven.

Cards: Normal pack used.

The deal: Each player is dealt six cards, three at a time.

The bidding: Starting with the player to the dealer's left, each player has one chance only to bid. The bid can be one, two, three or four, and represents the number of points the player hopes to achieve. Each bid must be higher than the previous one. Alternatively, a player can pass. If every player passes, the hand is redealt.

The highest bidder becomes the 'pitcher' for the hand.

The play: The pitcher leads to the first trick, and the suit led becomes trumps for the duration of the deal. Players must follow suit when trumps are led, or discard if they are unable to do so. However, when a non-trump suit is led, a player has the choice of following suit *or* trumping, even if he is able to follow. Obviously if he is void in the suit, he can discard.

The highest card of the suit led, or the highest trump if any have been played, wins the trick. The player winning the trick leads to the following one. The hand ends when all cards have been played.

The scoring: Points are scored, as in Seven-ups, for High, Low, Jack and Game, except that the point for Low is given to the player winning the trick containing the lowest trump, rather than the player dealt it.

The pitcher scores points only if he achieves his bid. Otherwise, he has the number bid deducted from his score (hence the name *Setback*). For example, if a player had a total of five points, bid three and made only two, his new total would be $5 - 3 = 2$.

It is quite feasible for a player to have a minus score, often referred to as being 'in the hole'.

Generally, a game of Auction pitch is played up to seven points.

Strategy: Because it is not compulsory to follow suit, except in the case of trumps, high cards in side-suits are less powerful than in most card games. It is important in the bidding to remain aware of this. Length is by far the most important feature of a potential trump suit, although three middling cards are not particularly helpful, as they provide little chance of a High or Low point.

The best policy for the pitcher will almost invariably be to draw trumps; in a way he is obliged to do so through his opening lead! This may provide him with an opportunity to set up tricks in his side-suits.

There are many variations on Auction pitch. Among them is **Smudge**, where any player achieving all four points in one hand automatically wins the game, regardless of the bid.

In **Joker pitch**, a Joker is added to the pack and becomes an additional trump, ranking below the lowest in the suit. It also becomes an additional point to play for, although the lowest true trump retains its status. There are thus five points available instead of the usual four.

A group of alternatives collectively known as **Pedro** uses different scoring systems, with various cards constituting additional points. The five and nine of trumps are often scored at their face values, with the total points required to win the game raised in parallel.

Whatever the nature of the variations, what sets Auction pitch apart from the early versions of All-fours is the skill and delicate sense of judgement required in the bidding, and the subsequent play of the cards.

Cinch

Possibly the most advanced game in the All-fours family is Cinch, also known as **High five** or **Double Pedro**. Like Auction pitch, it is widely played in the United States.

Number of players: Four, in two partnerships.

Cards: Normal pack used, however there is an extra trump card, the five of the same colour as the chosen trump suit. It ranks immediately below the five of trumps.

The deal: Each player is dealt nine cards, in groups of three.

The bidding: Starting with the player on the dealer's left, each player has one chance either to bid or pass, with each bid having to be higher than the previous one. The amount bid represents the number of points a player believes that he and his partner will make, given that he can choose the trump suit. Each trump held in tricks taken scores one point. Bids can range from one to fourteen. If everyone passes around to the dealer, he can either name trumps without making a bid, or he can pass. If everyone passes the cards are redealt.

Drawing and discarding: Once bidding has finished, the successful bidder names the trump suit. At this point all players bar the dealer discard unwanted cards, reducing their hands to six cards or less. They then draw from the stock until each player has six cards precisely.

The dealer is then at liberty to select from the remainder of the pack, plus his own hand, any six cards he chooses. Discards from his hand must be placed face up on the table, as must any trumps in the pack which he does not select.

The play: The successful bidder leads any card (not necessarily a trump). The play is as in Auction pitch (page 44), with the choice of following or trumping a non-trump lead, but with an obligation to follow in trumps where possible.

The scoring: If the partnership containing the successful bidder succeeds in making the number of points bid, the side with the higher count scores the difference between the two counts. Otherwise, the non-bidding partnership scores fourteen plus the number of points the bidding side fell short.

A couple of examples should clarify the situation.

If the bidding side call five, and make six points, this implies that the non-bidding side has made eight points. The non-bidding side therefore score $8 - 6 = 2$ points.

If the bidding side call six and make five points, the non-bidding side would score $14 + (6 - 5) = 15$ points.

A game of Cinch is played up to fifty-one points.

Strategy: Cinch is unusual in that even a successful bid can often result in one's opponents scoring points. For this reason, it is good policy to be very tentative in the bidding, particularly where the deal is with the opposite side.

There is a strong 'cat and mouse' element in the bidding, where it may often be best to accept a small sacrifice in order to prevent the opponents choosing their best suit.

The strategy in the play will be similar to Auction pitch (page 44).

There are many Cinch variations. It can be played as an individual rather than partnership game; alternatively, as in the game **Auction cinch**, the partnerships are not known until after the bidding is complete. Here, only six cards are dealt. The bidding takes place as in standard Cinch, then each player discards all unwanted cards before restoring his hand to six cards from stock. At this point, the successful bidder names a particular card, normally a trump, and the holder of that card acknowledges it and becomes the bidder's partner for the play.

In **Sixty-three** the scoring system is changed, with the King of trumps scoring twenty-five points, the 3 scoring fifteen, the 9 scoring nine, the two 5s scoring five apiece, the Ace, 10 and 2 scoring one point each, and all others worthless. Here, the highest possible bid is 63, and each game is played up to 152 points.

The Whist Family

Whist is one of the great card games, uncomplicated to learn, but virtually infinite in terms of the combinations and subtleties involved.

No one knows exactly when or how Whist came about. It is almost certainly a development from the earlier games of Triumph, from which the term 'trump' derived, and Ombre.

The simplicity of the game is reflected in the earliest known reference to Whist in 1674, with Charles Cotton refusing to include it in his *Compleat Gamester* on the grounds that 'every child of almost eight years old hath a competent knowledge in that recreation'.

Obviously Cotton failed to appreciate the hidden depths of Whist, and the skill required to play it well. Others did see its potential, none more so than Edmond Hoyle, who produced his book *A Short Treatise on the Game of Whist* in 1742. It turned out to be a bestseller, and the phrase 'according to Hoyle' became the ultimate authority on the rules of the game. Ironically, Hoyle himself was no great card player. He simply realized that Whist was a growing interest, and was able to capitalize on the market.

Towards the end of the nineteenth century Whist reached its peak in terms of popularity. Great minds turned to its scientific elements with Dr Henry Jones, better known as 'Cavendish', leading the way. Unfortunately his enthusiasm proved to be a false blessing. His written works were so complicated and mathematical that the average player was put off the game, and the popularity of Whist gradually declined.

Nowadays, Whist is played mainly as a social entertainment, at Whist Drives. Things have turned full circle. The people who attend Whist Drives are not generally great card players; they are people who enjoy it as a simple game, easily learnt but fun to play. Little do they realize that it was the complexities of Whist which killed it as the king of card games.

Whist

Number of players: Four, playing in two partnerships.

Cards: One normal pack is used.

The deal: All cards are dealt. The last card is turned up, and sets the trump suit. Once all the players have seen it, the dealer adds it to his hand.

Objective: Both partnerships attempt to win as many tricks as possible.

The play: The player to the dealer's left leads to the first trick. Each player contributes one card to the trick.

A player must follow suit if he is able to. Failure to do so is known as *revoking*, and is penalized in the scoring. If a player cannot follow suit, either he can discard or play a card from the trump suit.

The highest card played to a trick wins it, unless any trumps have been played, in which case the highest trump wins. The winner of a trick leads to the next one.

The hand ends when all the cards have been played.

Scoring: In the event of a player revoking, three points are awarded to the other side.

The partnership taking the majority of tricks is awarded one point for each trick over six. For example, if ten tricks are won, this scores four points.

Points are also awarded for honours. These are the top four cards in the suit designated as trumps. If a side holds all four honours, that is, Ace, King, Queen and Jack in the trump suit, four points are scored. Three honours score two points. If the honours are evenly divided, no points are scored for honours.

Each partnership strives to win a *rubber*, which comprises two games. A game is up to five points. Two bonus points are awarded for winning a rubber.

If a side already has four points, it is not entitled to claim for honours.

Strategy: The most important thing to remember is that Whist is a partnership game. The skill in Whist lies in the communication of information from one player to his partner, through the cards played during the course of the hand.

Cavendish produced thick books on this one topic alone, proposing that each card or sequence of cards would tell its own story. Without wishing to step into such murky depths, it is possible to lay down one or two guidelines.

1   *Opening lead* – this can tell your partner a great deal. Try to lead a suit that you would like your partner to lead back to you. Generally, this will be your longest suit. If you have touching honours, for example King and Queen, lead the higher of the two. Otherwise lead a low card. If you have a hand containing a number of trumps and one or two high cards, it is often sensible to lead a trump so as to drive out those held by your opponents.

2   *Returning partner's suit* – your partner will have led the suit that he wishes you to return. However, it is frequently possible to convey additional information by first playing a high card from your own strong suit. The more you know about each other's hands, the easier things become towards the end of the hand.

3 *Playing hints* – when playing to a trick second, it is best to play a low card, unless you are certain that you can win the trick. If you play high, you will often sacrifice potential winners.

Conversely, when playing third, it is best to play high, assuming your partner is not attempting to win the trick with his lead. Playing fourth, your choice will usually be obvious; either to win the trick with the lowest card possible, or to play low if your partner's card is winning or you cannot produce a higher card than your opponents.

These basic principles are best illustrated in a sample hand.

Sample Hand – Whist

There are four players, Norman, Sally, Eric and Wendy, sitting North, South, East and West respectively.

Sally deals, and turns up 7D to set the trump suit. The full deal is as follows:

S: Q, J, 10
H: 9, 7, 3
D: A, 9, 3
C: A, J, 9, 8

S: 9, 6
H: K, Q, 10, 4, 2
D: 10, 6, 5, 2
C: K, 3

N
W E
S

S: K, 7, 4, 3, 2
H: 8
D: J, 8, 4
C: Q, 7, 6, 5

S: A, 8, 5
H: A, J, 6, 5
D: K, Q, 7
C: 10, 4, 2

Wendy must lead to trick 1. She has an obvious opening lead, KH. This tells her partner, Eric, that hearts is her strong suit.

Trick 1: W leads KH, N plays 3H, E plays 8H, S wins with AH. *Trick count*: N/S 1   E/W 0. Sally must now find a suitable card to lead. Her best suit is hearts, but to lead one would, literally, be playing into Wendy's hands. Eventually she decides on 5S, although it is not an easy choice.

Trick 2: S leads 5S, W plays 6S, N plays 10S – note that any of the three spades would serve the same purpose; E plays KS and wins the trick. *Trick count*: N/S 1   E/W 1.

Eric has no hearts to lead back to Wendy. He decides on 5C, the lowest card in his longest suit.

Trick 3: E leads 5C, S plays 2C, W plays KC, N wins with AC. *Trick count*: N/S 2   E/W 1. Norman can now play QS, reasonably confident that it is a winner, since Sally would not have led spades without the Ace or King.

Trick 4: N leads QS, E plays 2S, S plays 8S, W plays 9S. *Trick count*: N/S 3   E/W 1. Norman now pauses to take stock of the situation. Eight spades have been played (two rounds of four cards), he has one left, and he assumes, incorrectly as it turns out, that Sally still has two. That leaves only two outstanding, so unless they are evenly distributed another spade lead might well be trumped. Therefore, in an attempt to set up the spades as winners, Norman decides to lead trumps so as to drive them out. He plays 3D.

Trick 5: N leads 3D, E plays 4D, S plays KD, W plays 2D. *Trick count*: N/S 4   E/W 1. Sally decides to continue the attack on trumps, leading QD.

Trick 6: S leads QD, W plays 5D, N plays 9D, E plays 8D. *Trick count*: N/S 5   E/W 1. Sally gives trumps one more go.

Trick 7: S leads 7D, W plays 6D, N plays AD, E plays JD. *Trick count*: N/S 6   E/W 1. Since there is only one trump still out, the chance of spades winning a trick now seems much brighter. Norman leads JS.

Trick 8: N leads JS, E plays 3S, S plays AS, W trumps with 10D. *Trick count*: N/S 6   E/W 2. Norman's plan has failed, but Wendy now has a difficult decision. Should she play QH, which she knows is a winner, or should she hold on in the hope that her partner Eric can lead a heart later on, possibly driving out a high card? She decides to play QH immediately, hoping JH will fall on the trick, thus setting up her 10H.

Trick 9: W leads QH, N plays 7H, E discards 6C – knowing that 7S and 4S are the only spades left, therefore winners; S plays 5H. *Trick count*: N/S 6   E/W 3. Wendy now leads a club, as requested by Eric at Trick 3.

Trick 10: W leads 3C, N plays 8C, E plays QC, S plays 4C. *Trick count*: N/S 6   E/W 4. Eric can now play his two winning spades.

Trick 11: E leads 7S, S discards 6H, W discards 2H, N discards 9H. *Trick count*: N/S 6   E/W 5.

Trick 12: E leads 4S, S discards JH – even though it is a winner, there is no point in keeping it since Sally knows, from Trick 9, that Eric has no hearts left to lead; W discards 4H, N discards 9C. *Trick count*: N/S 6   E/W 6.

Trick 13: E leads 7C, S plays 10C, W discards 10H, N plays JC. *Final trick count*: N/S 7   E/W 6.

Scoring: Norman and Sally have scored one point on the play, and two points for honours, holding AD, KD and QD between them.

I am sure that you can see possible improvements in the play. But remember that you can see all four hands; the players see only their own.

Whist as described above is the English version. As one might expect of such a classic game, there are numerous forms attributed to countries across the globe. There is American whist, Prussian whist, Norwegian whist, Russian whist, German whist and Chinese whist, to name but a few.

American whist is identical to the English game except for the scoring system. In America there are no points for honours, and a game is played up to seven points rather than five.

In **Prussian whist**, the American scoring system is used but trumps are determined not through turning the last card, but by cutting a second pack.

The other four versions differ more fundamentally, and are worth looking at in isolation.

♥ ♣ ♦ ♠

Norwegian Whist

Norwegian whist is unusual in that there are no trumps.

Number of players: Four, in two partnerships.

Cards: One normal pack is used.

The deal: All cards are dealt, thirteen to each player.

The bidding: There are two possible declarations: *Nullo*, in which case the objective is to win as few tricks as possible; or *Grand*, in which case the objective is to win as many tricks as possible. The player to the dealer's left has the first opportunity either to bid or pass. Once a bid is made the declaration is set, and no further bidding takes place. Otherwise the bidding rotates in a clockwise direction. If no one bids, the contract is 'nullo', with the dealer acting as declarer.

Obviously a bid must be made without knowledge of partner's cards. To a large extent it must be a gamble, based on the qualities of one's own hand.

The play: If the bid is Grand, the player to the declarer's right leads. If the bid is Nullo, the player to the declarer's left leads. Thereafter play continues in a clockwise direction.

A player must follow suit where possible, otherwise he must discard. The winner of a trick leads to the next one.

The hand ends when all cards have been played.

The scoring: In a bid of Grand, every trick over six scores four points; every trick under seven results in eight points being awarded to the non-bidding side.

In a bid of Nullo, every trick under seven scores two points; every trick over six results in two points being deducted from the bidding side, *and* two points being added to the non-bidders. The first side to reach fifty points wins.

The odds against a perfect hand in Whist, with all four players being dealt a complete suit, are:
2 235 197 406 895 366 301 599 999 to 1 against.

Put another way, if all the humans who had ever lived had spent all their lives dealing out cards, the odds are against such a hand ever having come up.

'Troy owes to Homer what Whist owes to Hoyle.'

Byron

Russian Whist

Also known as **Vint**, this game incorporates many of the attributes of Whist's most famous descendant, Bridge.

Number of players: Four, in two partnerships.

Cards: One normal pack is used.

The deal: All cards are dealt, thirteen to each player.

The bidding: Trumps are determined only after a sequence of bidding. The suits are ranked in the following order: no trumps (highest), hearts, diamonds, clubs and spades (lowest).

Each player bids in turn, starting with the dealer. The level of the bid indicates the number of tricks the bidder proposes to make above six, with the named suit as trumps. Therefore the lowest bid possible is One Spade (proposing to make seven tricks with spades as trumps), and the highest is Seven No Trumps proposing to make every trick with no trumps.

A player can bid or pass, with each bid being higher than the previous one.

It is perfectly legitimate for a player to overcall his partner's bid, even with the opposition silent.

The bidding concludes after three successive passes.

The play: The player to the successful bidder's left leads to the first trick. Thereafter play rotates in a clockwise direction.

A player must follow suit where possible, otherwise he can trump or discard. The winner of a trick leads to the next one.

The hand ends when all cards have been played.

The scoring: A Russian whist scoresheet has two columns, one for each side, with a horizontal line enabling points to be scored 'above' and 'below' the line.

A + B	C + D

Points are scored below the line for each trick taken by both sides, regardless of the bidding. The value of the trick depends on the level of the bid. A bid of 'one' gives a trick value of 10; a bid of 'two' gives a trick value of 20; and so on up to a bid of 'seven' and a corresponding trick value of 70. 500 points below the line constitute a game, with two games making up a rubber.

Bonus points, scored above the line, are awarded as follows:

One game in an unfinished rubber: 1000.
Winning a rubber: 2000.
Twelve tricks (a *little slam*) made but not bid 1000, if bid 6000.
Thirteen tricks (a *grand slam*), not bid 2000, bid 12000.

Points for honours are also scored above the line. The honours cards are the Ace, King, Queen and Jack of trumps, plus the other Aces; the Ace of trumps scores twice, as a top trump and an Ace. In a no-trump contract, only the four Aces are honours.

If one side has the majority of honours and Aces, it scores ten times the level of the bid for each honour. For example, if a partnership holds three Aces and three honours, and the contract is Three Clubs, the honours points would be $3 \times 10 \times 6 = 180$.

If one side has the majority of honours, whilst the other has the majority of Aces, the two are compared, the lower value is deducted from the higher, and that figure is used in the honours calculation. For example, if one side has four trump honours but only one Ace (the Ace of trumps), while the other has no trump honours and the other three Aces, the first will score for two honours only $(5 - 3)$. If, as above, the contract was Three Clubs, the honour count would be $10 \times 3 \times 2 = 60$.

At no trumps, the side holding the most Aces scores 25 times the trick value for each Ace held. For example, if three Aces were held, and the contract was Four No Trumps, the honours count would be $25 \times 3 \times 4 = 300$.

If the Aces are evenly divided between the partnerships in a no-trump contract, no honours points are scored; if the Aces are evenly divided in a trump contract, the side winning the most tricks is entitled to claim honours. For example, if each side held two Aces, and the first side scored nine tricks in a contract of Two Hearts, they could claim $2 \times 10 \times 2 = 40$ honours points.

Any one player holding three Aces, or a sequence of three cards headed by an Ace, can claim 500 honours points. This is known as a *coronet*. If the coronet is in the trump suit, or the hand is being played in no trumps, the bonus is doubled to 1000 points. Also, any additional card in the sequence adds 500 points to its value. For example, if a player held A, K, Q, J, 10, 9 in a suit other than trumps, this would score $500 + (500 \times 3) = 2000$ points.

Finally, if a partnership has failed to fulfil its bid, it is penalized by 100 times the trick value for each undertrick, while simultaneously being rewarded for the tricks which have been made. The penalties for undertricks are scored above the line. For example, if Side 1 bid Four Spades (giving a trick value of 40) and made eight tricks, thus incurring two undertricks, the scoring would be as follows:

Side 1: 8 × 40 = 320 points below the line.
Side 2: 5 × 40 = 200 points below; 2 × 40 × 100 = 800 points above.

Strategy: The bidding is crucial. It is certainly desirable to bid a hand up to its limits, but the enormous penalties for failing to fulfil a contract must be borne in mind. Much will depend on the state of the score; when you are close to a game, it may be worth playing safe.

Since points are accumulated below the line during the course of the hand, a game may well be concluded before the hand itself is completed. Sometimes the play of the cards can be geared towards this eventuality.

56

German Whist

This member of the Whist family employs the 'draw' principle, with each player taking cards from a stock pile during the course of play.

Number of players: Two.

Cards: One normal pack is used.

The deal: Six cards are dealt to each player, then the top card of stock is turned up, and sets the trump suit.

The play: The non-dealer leads to the first trick. The winner of the trick takes the top card, in this case the card turned up as trumps, while the loser of the trick takes the second card from stock. The new top card of stock is now turned up.

Play continues in this way, with the players' hands being continually replenished from stock, and with the top card of the stock pile continually being turned up.

Once the stock pile is exhausted, the players play out their remaining cards, and count up the number of tricks each has won. The hand is tied if each has won thirteen tricks, otherwise the player taking the most tricks has won.

Strategy: The fact that both players know what the next card is dictates the tactics for each trick. If it is a good card, they will attempt to win the trick. If it is a poor one, there is no point in wasting a top card.

It is usually worth trying to win a trick when the top card is a trump, regardless of its value.

Chinese Whist

Unlike the other Whist games described, the players in Chinese whist are able to plan their play with a fairly comprehensive knowledge of each others' cards.

Number of players: Four, in two partnerships.

Cards: One normal pack is used.

The deal: Each player is dealt six cards, face down. Six further cards are then dealt, face up on top of the first cards. Each player is then dealt a single 'playing' card.

Naming trumps: The dealer examines his hand then names the trump suit.

The play: The player to the dealer's left leads to the first trick, using either his concealed 'playing' card, or one of the face-up cards on the table. Each player must then contribute to the trick, following suit where possible, playing only from the face-up cards or the concealed card. As the face-up cards are played, the face-down ones beneath are turned over, and become available for play.

The hand ends when all the cards have been played.

Scoring: This is exactly the same as for standard Whist (page 51)

58

A Chinese whist hand in progress.

Solo Whist

This is one of the most interesting and popular members of the Whist family. Often abbreviated simply to **Solo**, it incorporates the element of deliberate trick-losing, so that even if you hold a really poor hand, there is still plenty to play for. There is also a three-handed version of Solo, in case someone forgets to turn up!

Number of players: Four.

Cards: One normal pack is used.

The deal: Thirteen cards are dealt to each player, in four groups of three, and a single card on the last round. The last card in the dealer's hand is turned up, to indicate the potential trump suit.

The bidding: Each player, starting from the left of the dealer, has the opportunity to bid or pass. Each bid must be higher than the previous one. The order of bids, and their respective meanings, are as follows:

1   *Prop and Cop* – a call of 'Prop' indicates that the bidder is prepared to try and make eight tricks in partnership with any of the other three, with trumps determined by the upturned card. If there are no higher, intervening bids, one of the other players can, in his turn, call 'Cop', which confirms the partnership.

2   *Solo* – the bidder will attempt to make five tricks, using the trump suit indicated by the upturned card, and playing against the other three players.

3   *Misere* – the bidder proposes to lose every trick, playing with no trump suit.

4   *Abundance* – the bidder will attempt to make nine tricks, with his own preferred trump suit, which is announced only after all the other players have passed.

5   *Royal Abundance* – the bidder will attempt to make nine tricks, using the trump suit indicated by the upturned card.

6   *Open Misere* – the bidder will attempt to lose every trick, playing with his hand face-up after the first trick.

7   *Declared Abundance* – the bidder proposes to win all thirteen tricks, playing with no trump suit. The bidding continues until no one is prepared to go any higher.

The play: The player to the dealer's left leads, except in the case of Declared Abundance, when the successful bidder leads.

The play is as in standard Whist, except that a hand need not be completed if a player has fulfilled his bid, or if a trick has been taken by a player attempting Misere.

The scoring: Solo is best played for gambling chips, although scores can be kept on paper.

If a Prop and Cop contract is fulfilled, one of the successful partners is paid five chips by one opponent, while the other member of the successful partnership is paid five chips by the other opponent. If the contract is not fulfilled, the payments are reversed.

Each of the other bids has a standard value. If successful, the caller is paid the set amount by each of the other players. Otherwise, he must pay the set

Bid	Requirement	Points
Prop and Cop	8 tricks in partnership	5
Solo	5 tricks, indicated suit	10
Misere	0 tricks, no trumps	15
Abundance	9 tricks, preferred suit	20
Royal Abundance	9 tricks, indicated suit	20
Open Misere	0 tricks, hand exposed	30
Declared Abundance	13 tricks, no trumps	40

amount to them. The scoring, and a brief summary of the bids, is shown above.
Strategy: The bidding requirements for trick-taking contracts are fairly obvious; a good holding in trumps, whether indicated or preferred, and a fair selection of high cards.

For Misere the situation is less clear-cut. It is possible to succeed in losing every trick even if one or two high cards are held. A void suit, one in which you possess no cards, is particularly useful. Most importantly, you must have at least one low card in every suit that you do hold cards in.

It is always worth bearing in mind that the distribution of cards around the table is likely to be uneven, because of the style of dealing.

The play varies dramatically according to the call. A player bidding Misere must attempt to ditch potential winners, while his opponents keep low cards back so as to 'throw him in'.

Defending is a subtle art in Solo. In most cases, where you are playing three against one, it is best to try and lead through the caller. This means that the caller should be made to play second or third, rather than fourth. The reasons, as outlined in the Playing Hints for standard Whist (page 50), are as follows. If he is fourth (and last) to play to a trick, he knows exactly which card to play in order to win or lose the trick. If there is one or more players to follow, he is faced with a much more difficult decision.

Try to keep track of the cards. Often the crucial moment in a hand comes towards the end, and there is nothing worse than being forced to make a vital decision when you have totally forgotten everything that has gone before.

There are those who feel that Solo is a slightly restrictive game, because the bids are limited such that a player is always attempting to make no tricks, five tricks, nine tricks or thirteen tricks; or eight in partnership with another player.

If you feel this way, you may prefer **Auction solo**. In addition to the standard Solo bids, there are six-, seven- and eight-trick 'Solo' calls available, and ten-, eleven- and twelve-trick 'Abundance' calls. Each bid has two categories, either with the proposed trump suit as turned up in the deal, or with trumps named by the successful bidder. The proposed trump suit has precedence. For example, if a spade had been turned up, then a six-trick Solo with spades as trumps would be a higher bid than a six-trick Solo with diamonds as trumps.

The scoring is as in standard Solo, with no additional credit being given for higher calls. Thus an eight-trick Solo would score ten points, exactly the same as a standard five-trick Solo. The auction element merely allows more competitiveness in the bidding.

For **Three-handed solo** the pack is reduced to forty cards, with the twos, threes, and fours stripped out. Thirty-nine cards are dealt, with the fortieth proposing trumps.

Obviously the Prop and Cop bid no longer applies, and the order of bids changes, with Misere outranking Abundance, and Open Misere outranking Declared Abundance. Similarly, their respective scores are inverted: Misere scores twenty points, Open Misere scores forty, Abundance scores fifteen and Declared Abundance scores thirty.

Boston

Boston is a very close relative of Solo whist, and although it is less frequently played, it may well be an earlier game. Certainly it was popular at the time of the American Revolution.

Number of players: Four, each playing as an individual.

Cards: Two normal packs, one for play, one to determine trumps.

The deal: Thirteen cards are dealt to each player, four groups of three followed by a single card.

The bidding: The second pack is cut, and the top card of the bottom section is turned up to set the *preference* suit. The other suit of the same colour is known as the *colour* suit. For example, if the preference suit is spades, the colour suit will be clubs. The other two are *plain* suits.

Bidding starts with the player to the dealer's left, then each player in turn can bid or pass, with each bid higher than the previous one. The ranking of bids is as follows:

1   To win five tricks (*Boston*).
2   To win six tricks.
3   To win seven tricks.
4   To lose twelve tricks, with each player discarding one card (*Little Misery*); there are no trumps.
5   To win eight tricks.
6   To win nine tricks.
7   To lose every trick in no trumps (*Grand Misery*).
8   To win ten tricks.
9   To win eleven tricks.
10   To lose twelve tricks, as in Little Misery, but with your hand exposed (*Little Spread*); there are no trumps.
11   To win twelve tricks.
12   To lose every trick, but with your hand exposed (*Grand Spread*); there are no trumps.
13   To win all thirteen tricks (*Grand Slam*).

For each of the positive bids, the suits are ranked in descending order: preference, colour, plain. Thus in the example given, six tricks in spades outranks six tricks in clubs, which in turn outranks six tricks in hearts or diamonds.

The bidding concludes when three successive players pass.

The play: The player to the dealer's left leads. The play of the cards is identical to standard Whist, except that a hand need not be played out if a bid has been fulfilled, or if a trick has been taken by a player who is attempting Misery or Spread.

The scoring: Boston is best played for gambling chips; alternatively a record can be kept on paper.

A bidder who fulfils his contract is paid a number of chips by each of the other players, corresponding to the following table:

Tricks bid	5	6	7	8	9	10	11	12	13
Chips paid	2	3	4	5	7	9	13	21	34

A bidder who fails to fulfil a contract must pay each opponent a given amount according to the number of tricks by which he falls short, and the level of the contract. The payments are as follows:

Tricks bid	*Tricks fallen short*												
	1	2	3	4	5	6	7	8	9	10	11	12	13
5	2	4	6	8	10								
6	3	5	7	9	11	13							
7	4	6	8	10	12	14	16						
8	5	7	9	11	14	17	20	23					
9	7	9	11	13	16	19	22	25	28				
10	9	11	14	16	19	22	25	28	31	34			
11	14	16	19	22	25	28	31	34	37	40	44		
12	24	26	29	32	36	40	44	48	52	56	60	64	
13	36	40	44	48	52	56	60	64	68	72	78	84	90

It is usual for a group of players to have a common pot, to which everyone contributes before a deal. The pot is allowed to accumulate until a player fulfils a bid of seven or more. That player then wins the pot, in addition to the standard payments from his opponents.

The rewards and punishments for succeeding or failing at a Misery or Spread contract are identical; four chips for Little Misery, eight for Grand Misery, sixteen for Little Spread, and thirty-two for Grand Spread. The bidder pays or collects depending on the outcome of the contract.

Oh Hell!

Also known as **Blackout**, this is a fun game for any number of players.

Number of players: Three or more.

Cards: One normal pack is used.

The deal: The top card is turned up to determine trumps for the hand, then the pack is reshuffled. The cards are dealt out, the same number to each player. If an uneven number is left at the end of the deal, the remaining are put aside, unseen.

The bidding: Each player declares how many tricks he intends to win, anything from zero to every trick.

The play: The player to the dealer's left leads, thereafter play is identical to standard whist.

The scoring: A player is awarded one point for every trick taken, and a bonus of ten if he takes exactly the number of tricks he had declared. A player who has declared zero and succeeds in taking no tricks receives ten points precisely.

A game is played up to 100 points.

Strategy: You need to employ 'cat and mouse' tactics in Oh Hell! You must strive to make your own declaration, whilst trying to prevent other players making theirs. Which objective should take precedence depends largely on the total score.

Bridge

Without a doubt, Bridge is the undisputed heavyweight champion in the world of card games. If you looked in your local library in the appropriate section, you would find that at least nine out of every ten books on cards are in fact books on Bridge.

It is a relatively recent game, certainly in the western hemisphere, where the first references are around the turn of the century. However its origins are much earlier. It is believed that Bridge originated in Russia, where it is known as *Biritch*, although its passage to Britain may well have been via India.

At first Bridge was rarely played, and its elderly relative Whist continued to hold centre stage. But gradually things changed and as Whist, in the hands of Cavendish, became more and more complicated, card players turned to Bridge, which they felt was more exciting and less intellectually draining.

The first form of the game was Straight bridge, in which trumps were nominated either by the dealer or his partner. Then came Auction bridge, where everyone could bid for trumps. Finally, around 1925, Contract bridge emerged, or simply Bridge as it is now known universally. The main difference between Contract and Auction bridge is the scoring method.

Along the way several innovations were tried. Some, like the no trump bid, remain. Others, such as a nullo bid where the declarer would attempt to lose tricks rather than win them, soon died.

Various experiments also took place with the scoring, but eventually a system was settled on and the result is Bridge as we know it.

It is impossible to deal with so massive a subject in so little space. All I can attempt to do is to give a brief outline of the game, and its principal elements. If you wish to play Bridge well, it will be necessary to search out a more specialized book.

Number of players:　Four, in two partnerships. These are determined by drawing cards from a face-down pack. The two players drawing the two highest cards form one partnership; the two players drawing the two lowest cards form the other.

Cards:　One normal pack is used. In order to speed things up, it is usual to have a second pack which can be shuffled, ready for the next deal, while the first is being dealt.

The deal:　The player who drew the highest card is dealer for the first hand, thereafter the deal rotates clockwise.

The player to the dealer's left shuffles the pack, the player to the dealer's right cuts it, and the dealer's partner shuffles the second pack in readiness for the following deal.

All cards are dealt, thirteen to each player.

The bidding: Trumps are determined only after a sequence of bidding. The suits are ranked in the following order: No trumps (highest), spades, hearts, diamonds, clubs (lowest).

Each player bids in turn, starting with the dealer. The level of the bid indicates the number of tricks the bidder's partnership proposes to make above six, with the suit named as trumps. Therefore the lowest bid is One Club (proposing to make seven tricks with clubs as trumps), the highest Seven No Trumps (proposing to make thirteen tricks with no trumps).

A player has the choice either of bidding or passing, with each bid being higher than the previous one.

If all four players pass initially, the cards are thrown in and a new hand is dealt by the next dealer.

At any stage, a player can *double* any bid made by his opponents. This generally means that he does not believe that they can fulfil their contract, and he proposes that any scores or penalties on the hand should be doubled. A member of the first partnership can now redouble, indicating confidence that the contract is sound, and proposing that the scores should be doubled up a second time.

A double or redouble can be overbid by the next standard bid in the sequence. For example, a sequence of bids such as 'Two Spades – Double – Redouble – Two No Trumps' is perfectly valid.

After three successive passes, the last bid made becomes the contract, and the player who first mentioned the suit in which the contract is to be played becomes the *declarer*.

The principles of bidding are best illustrated in a sample deal:

S K,Q,10,8,5
H: K, 10, 5
D: 8, 2
C: 9, 7, 2

S: 9, 6, 4, 3
H: Q, 8, 4
D: K, Q, J, 4
C: 6, 4

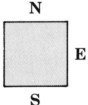

S: A, J, 7
H: 7, 6
D: 9, 7, 6
C: K, Q, J, 8, 3

S: 2
H: A, J, 9, 3, 2
D: A, 10, 5, 3
C: A, 10, 5

South is the dealer. The bidding is as follows:

South	West	North	East
1H	Pass	1S	2C
2D	Double	2H	Pass
Pass	Pass		

South's bids have shown a reasonable hand with the best two suits being hearts and diamonds.

West doubled South's bid in diamonds, because he felt that his strength in diamonds would prevent South making eight tricks with diamonds as trumps.

North has shown a good spade suit, and a preference for hearts rather than diamonds.

East's bid has indicated a fair hand with a strong club suit.

In the end, the North/South partnership has contracted to make eight tricks with hearts as trumps. South is the declarer, since he mentioned hearts first.

The play: The player to the declarer's left leads to the first trick.

As soon as the opening lead is on the table, the declarer's partner places his hand on the table, trumps on his right. He now takes no further part in the play, and he and his cards are referred to as the *dummy*. In the example above, North is the dummy.

The declarer has sole control of the dummy, choosing which cards should be played to each trick.

The rules for play are as in standard Whist, with dummy's cards being played in strict rotation, and with the winner of each trick leading to the next.

Tricks won by the declarer are gathered and placed in front of him. Tricks won by the opponents, known as the *defence*, are gathered and placed in front of either player. The number of tricks won by each side should always be clearly visible.

A trick cannot be looked at once the next lead has been made.

The hand ends when all cards have been played.

The scoring: A Bridge scoresheet has two columns, for *We* and *They*, and a horizontal line enabling points to be scored above and below the line.

In the 1930s, an attempt was made to introduce a fifth suit to Bridge. Known as 'royals' it was represented by a crown, and ranked above spades. The attempt failed; players found Bridge quite challenging enough with four suits!

WE	THEY
30	
60	

Only tricks contracted for and successfully made are scored below the line. The trick value varies for the different suits. Spades and hearts are worth thirty points per trick. Diamonds and clubs are worth twenty points per trick. In no trumps, the first trick scores forty points, while subsequent tricks are worth thirty points apiece.

Everything else is scored above the line: overtricks, honours, bonuses and penalties for unfulfilled contracts.

Overtricks are additional tricks made above the level of the contract. They are scored at the normal trick value. For example, if the sample hand above resulted in nine tricks being won by North/South, this would be scored as sixty points below the line (thirty points for each trick above six which has been bid and successfully made) plus thirty points above the line for the unbid overtrick.

The honours cards are Ace, King, Queen, Jack and 10 of trumps, or the four Aces in a no-trump contract. Possession of four of the five trump honours in one hand scores 100 bonus, possession of all five scores 150. Possession of all four Aces in one hand in a no-trump contract scores 150 bonus.

Other bonus points available are for rubbers and slams. A *rubber* is won by the first side to make two games, where a game comprises 100 points below the line. A game can be made in several hands, or in a single hand if the bid is high enough. Bids such as Three No Trumps (worth 100 points) or Four Spades (worth 120 points) are known as *game bids*.

If a partnership wins a rubber without their opponents making a game, the bonus is 700 points. If both sides have made games, the bonus is 500 points.

When a partnership has won a game, they are said to be *vulnerable*, and the corresponding penalties for failing to fulfil a contract are higher. So too are the bonuses for bidding and making *slam* contracts. A *little slam* is twelve tricks bid for and made. A non-vulnerable little slam scores 500, vulnerable it scores

750. A *grand slam* is all thirteen tricks bid for and made. Non-vulnerable, a grand slam scores 1000, vulnerable it scores 1500.

Penalties for failing to make a contract are as follows: non-vulnerable, each trick by which a contract falls short is worth fifty penalty points to the defence; vulnerable, the penalty is 100 points per trick. For example, if a partnership bid Four Hearts and made eight tricks, the penalty would be 100 points non-vulnerable, 200 points vulnerable.

Doubling and redoubling affects the scoring radically. For the declarer, the trick values in a successful doubled contract are themselves doubled, and in addition a bonus of fifty points is scored above the line. Should the declarer be fortunate enough to make overtricks in a doubled contract, the rewards are even greater, 100 points for a non-vulnerable overtrick, 200 points for a vulnerable overtrick.

WE	THEY
700	
50	
200	
120	
180	

For example, consider that declarer is vulnerable, and plays in a contract of Three Spades doubled. He makes ten tricks. Therefore his side scores 180 points below the line (30 × 3 all doubled) + 200 points above the line for the overtrick, 50 points for the insult of being doubled, and 700 points for winning the rubber, assuming the opponents have not won a game.

Redoubling, as one might expect, results in each of the above figures being doubled up once more, apart from the 50 bonus and 700 for rubber.

When your partner has just led the wrong card, and allowed your opponents to make a wholly unmakeable slam, just remember: 'It's only a game!'

Just as success in a doubled contract is rewarded more lucratively, failure is punished more severely. Non-vulnerable, the first undertrick produces a 100-point penalty and subsequent undertricks are worth 200 points. Vulnerable, the figures are 200 points for a one-trick penalty, 300 points for subsequent tricks.

For example, if one side were vulnerable and bid Three Clubs, which their opponents doubled, and the contract made seven tricks, the penalty would be $200 + 300 = 500$ points for the defence.

Redoubled penalties are precisely twice doubled penalties.

PROBABILITY OF CARD HOLDINGS IN A 13-CARD BRIDGE HAND			
Type of hand	Number of these hands*	Probability (%)	Approximate odds against drawing
Four aces	1 677 106 640	0.26	378 to 1
No aces	192 928 249 296	30.4	7 to 3
No card higher than a nine (Yarborough)	347 373 603	0.055	1 827 to 1
Seven-card suit or longer	25 604 567 408	4.03	24 to 1
Any 4–3–3–3 distribution	6.691×10^{10}	10.54	17 to 2
Any 5–4–2–2 distribution	6.718×10^{10}	10.58	17 to 2
Any 5–3–3–2 distribution	9.853×10^{10}	15.52	11 to 2

*Out of a total of 635 013 559 600 possible hands.

Scientific Bridge players continually experiment with new bidding systems, where nothing means exactly what it appears to mean. One recent development is the 'forcing pass', where the opening bidder informs his partner that he has a strong hand by refusing to bid!

The Bezique Family

Bezique is a two-player, two-pack game which became extremely popular in the middle of the nineteenth century. Originally it was played only in Europe, other nations being slow to catch on to its attractions. However, as had happened before and would happen again, it took a member of the royal family to popularize the game in Britain. In this case it was Queen Victoria's son Alfred, Duke of Edinburgh, who came across Bezique on his travels, and became an addict.

There are many forms; the original, reputedly invented by Swedish schoolmaster Gustav Flaker, is examined overleaf.

Bezique

Number of players: Two.

Cards: Two 32-card packs (6 – 2 stripped out) are shuffled together, to form a 64-card double-pack. The cards are ranked, in descending order, Ace (highest), 10, K, Q, J, 9, 8, 7 (lowest) – note the unusual position of the 10. The Ace and 10 are known as *brisque* cards.

Objective: To score points by making declarations (see below) and by winning tricks containing brisque cards.

The deal: Eight cards are dealt to each player, in groups of three, two and three. The next is turned up to set trumps, and the remainder form a stock pile. If a 7 is turned up, the dealer receives ten points.

The play: There are two distinct phases of play, the Declaration stage and the Playoff.

Declaration stage: The main objective during this phase is to collect cards such that certain scoring combinations can be formed. They are:

Name	Requirement	Points
Common marriage	K–Q of a plain suit	20
Royal marriage	K–Q of trumps	40
Bezique	QS and JD	40
Forty Jacks	Any four Jacks	40
Sixty Queens	Any four Queens	60
Eighty Kings	Any four Kings	80
Hundred Aces	Any four Aces	100
Sequence	A, 10, K, Q, J of trumps	250
Double bezique	QS–JD–QS–JD	500

These combinations are valueless until they can be declared. The building of combinations and their declaration takes place as follows:

The non-dealer leads to the first trick; thereafter the winner of the previous trick leads. The second player can follow suit, discard or play a trump – in other words he can play any card he chooses to. The trick is won by the highest card of the suit led, or the highest trump. If both players play identical cards, the player who led wins the trick.

After winning a trick a player may make a declaration. He lays, face-down, any of the combinations mentioned above. These still count as cards within his hand, and can be played in subsequent tricks or used to construct new combinations. The following rules apply to declarations:

1   A declaration can only be made by a player immediately after winning a trick. It is no good holding the cards for a high-scoring combination – you must win a trick in order to make a declaration and score for it.

2   Only one declaration can be made at a time.

3 Cards already played to tricks cannot be used in declarations.
4 Cards which are on the table within declared combinations can be reused, but only in a different combination.
5 A marriage contained within a sequence cannot be declared.
6 A card cannot be added to a quartet (four-of-a-kind) and re-scored as a new quartet.
7 It is not possible to break down combinations to form others, whereas it is perfectly legitimate to build up combinations, scoring at each stage.

A few examples should clarify the situation. If you have four Kings and four Queens on the table, you could then declare a common marriage or royal marriage after next winning a trick because you are taking the cards for the marriage from two *different* combinations; similarly, you could extract a card from your hand to combine with one on the table. This is an example of Rule 4.

However, if you held A–10–K–Q–J of trumps (a sequence) on the table, you could not claim a royal marriage, because both King and Queen are within the *same* combination nor could you claim a Royal Marriage after playing off A–10–J. This illustrates Rules 5 and 7.

If you had declared a double bezique, you could not then score forty points for each of the individual beziques within it. However, if you declared one bezique, you could then declare a second, followed by a double bezique. This would be worth 580 points, but would necessitate winning three tricks. Again, these are examples of Rule 7.

After adding the points scored for any declarations, the player winning the trick takes the top card from stock, and the player losing it takes the second card from stock.

Play continues until the stock is exhausted. The winner of the last trick takes the last card of stock, the loser taking the turned-up trump.

At any stage, the player holding a trump 7 can declare it, winning ten points.

Playoff stage: Once stock is exhausted, phase two commences. The cards on the table are replaced in the players' hands, and play continues with slightly different rules for trick-taking. It is now compulsory to follow suit if possible, and trump or discard if it is not. A trick must be won where a card is held which can win it.

Scoring: As well as the points accumulated during the declaration stage, ten points are awarded for winning the last trick, and ten points for each brisque card held in all tricks taken during both phases.

A game of Bezique is played up to 1000 points.

Strategy: Most of the points in a game of Bezique come from declarations rather then the successful capture of brisque cards. Therefore your strategy should reflect this.

During the first phase, there is really no need to win tricks unless you wish to make a declaration. Your objective should be to discard worthless cards, 7s, 8s and 9s, while retaining a few likely winners should you wish to declare. Because there is no requirement to follow suit, a few trumps can usually be regarded as likely winners.

When you have no worthless cards, consider the Jacks dispensable, since

73

four Jacks are really not worth saving for. But *never* use JD, unless you have already seen both QS appear.

Sometimes you will find yourself with promising combinations from which there appears to be no convenient discard. If this is the case, examine the cards declared on the table, and try to remember which cards have been played in tricks. A promising combination can soon become useless if the cards required to complete it appear in a declaration of your opponent. It is generally better to play cards from the table rather than from hand, because you are not then giving away unknown information.

Finally, don't be greedy. If you hold a double bezique, and cannot guarantee winning three tricks, then declare it immediately rather than hoping to declare each part separately.

Sample Hand – Bezique

This is not the simplest of games to follow. I would suggest that you lay out the cards face-up, then play the hand through.

The two players are Anneka and Boris. Anneka deals, and the cards come out as follows:

	Anneka	Boris
Spades	A, A, K, J	10, 9
Hearts	10	A, 9, 9, 8
Diamonds	A	K
Clubs	J, 9	A

The card turned up is 10D, setting diamonds as trumps.

Trick 1: Boris leads 8H, Anneka plays 10H, winning the trick. Anneka picks 7H, Boris picks JS.

Trick 2: Anneka leads 9C, Boris discards 9H. Anneka picks QD, Boris picks 8S.

Trick 3: Anneka leads 7H, Boris discards 8S. Anneka picks KC, Boris picks JD.

Trick 4: Anneka leads JS, Boris wins with 10S. He now picks 8S, Anneka picks JC.

Their hands are now as follows:

> *Anneka*   **S:** A, A, K   **H:**–   **D:** A, Q   **C:** K, J, J
> *Boris*   **S:** J, 9, 8   **H:** A, 9   **D:** K, J   **C:** A

Anneka needs only an Ace for a Hundred Aces, as she did at the start, but she is struggling for discards. Boris has no such hopes, or problems!

Trick 5: Boris leads 8S, Anneka discards JC. Boris picks 9S, Anneka picks 10D.

Trick 6: Boris leads 9S, Anneka discards JC. Boris picks QD, Anneka picks 7C.

Trick 7: Boris leads 9H, Anneka discards 7C. Boris now declares a royal marriage, K–Q of diamonds. He picks KC, while Anneka picks JH.
The score is Anneka 0, Boris 40.

Trick 8: Boris leads 9S, Anneka discards JH. Boris picks KD, Anneka picks QC.

Trick 9: Boris leads JS, Anneka wins with KS, and declares a marriage in clubs. Anneka picks 10C, Boris AD.
The score is now Anneka 20, Boris 40, and their hands are:

> *Anneka*   **S:** A, A   **H:** –   **D:** A, 10, Q   **C:** 10; with KC, QC on table.
> *Boris*   **S:** –   **H:** A   **D:** A, K, J   **C:** A, K; with KD, QD on table.

Trick 10: Anneka leads 10C, Boris plays KC. Boris picks QC, Anneka picks 8H.

Trick 11: Boris leads QC, Anneka discards 8H. Boris picks 7S, Anneka picks KS.

Trick 12: Boris leads 7S, Anneka discards QC from the table. Boris picks JD, Anneka picks 8D.

Trick 13: Boris leads KD from the table, Anneka discards KC, also from the table. Boris picks 10C, Anneka picks QH. Their hands now are:

> *Anneka*   **S:** A, A, K   **H:** Q   **D:** A, 10, Q, 8   **C:** –
> *Boris*   **S:** –   **H:** A   **D:** A, K, J, J   **C:** A, 10; with QD on table.

Trick 14: Boris leads 10C, Anneka trumps with 8D. Anneka picks 10H, Boris picks 9D.

Trick 15: Anneka leads 10H, Boris trumps with 9D. Boris picks 9C, Anneka picks 7C.

Trick 16: Boris leads 9C, Anneka plays 7C. Boris picks JH, Anneka picks QS.

Trick 17: Boris leads JH, Anneka plays QH, winning the trick. Anneka now declares a marriage in spades. Anneka picks 10S and Boris QS. The scores are now tied at 40 each, with the players holding the following cards:

> *Anneka*   **S:** A, A, 10   **H:** –   **D:** A, 10, Q   **C:** –; with KS, QS on table.
> *Boris*   **S:** Q   **H:** A   **D:** A, K, J, J   **C:** A; with QD on table.

Trick 18: Anneka leads 10S and Boris trumps with JD. He can afford to let it go because, having seen Anneka's QS, he knows that he has no chance of a double-bezique. He declares his single bezique, then picks 9D, while Anneka picks AC.
The score is now 80–40 in Boris's favour.

Trick 19: Boris leads 9D, which Anneka takes with 10D – having seen both JD appear, she has given up hope of a sequence. She declares a hundred Aces, making the score 140–80 in her favour. She picks KH, and Boris picks AH.

Trick 20: Anneka leads KS from table, which Boris trumps with JD, also from table. He can now declare his hundred Aces and restore his lead. He picks 7D and Anneka picks 8D. Their hands are:

> *Anneka*   In hand, KH and QD, 8D; on table, AS, AS, AD, AC and QS.
> *Boris*   In hand, KD, 7D; on table, AD, AH, AH, AC, QS and QD.

Trick 21: Boris leads 7D, claiming 10 points. Anneka plays 8D, winning the trick. Anneka picks 7S, Boris picks KH.

The score is now Anneka 140, Boris 90.

Trick 22: Anneka leads 7S, Boris wins with QS from table. Boris picks QH, Anneka picks 7H.

Trick 23: There is just time for Boris to declare his marriage in hearts. He leads AD from table, to ensure that he wins the trick. Anneka discards 7H. Boris declares his marriage, then both players pick 8C. Score: 140–210.

Trick 24: The two 8Cs are played, with Boris taking the last card from stock, 7D, while Anneka gets the 10D turned up.

The Playoff

The players are now ready for the final eight tricks. They replace the cards from the table into their hands:

> *Anneka*   **S:** A, A, Q   **H:** K   **D:** A, 10, Q   **C:** A
> *Boris*   **S:** –   **H:** A, A, K, Q   **D:** K, Q, 7   **C:** A

Boris leads AC, which wins. He follows with AH, followed by his second AH. This is trumped with QD by Anneka. She leads AS, which Boris trumps with 7D, claiming his second ten-point bonus. The last four tricks comprise Boris's two last hearts, trumped by Anneka, and Anneka's two spades, trumped by Boris. Boris wins the last trick and the ten-point bonus.

The players count up their brisque cards, for which Anneka scores sixty points and Boris 100. Thus the total score on the hand is Anneka 200 (140 + 60); Boris 210 (100 + 110).

Standard Bezique can be played perfectly well with three players. An extra 32-card pack is used. The rules for play are exactly the same, but with a triple bezique scoring 1500 points.

If you own sufficient packs of cards, you may like to try one or two of the multi-pack variants.

Rubicon Bezique

Number of players: Two.

Cards: Four 32-card packs are used, making up 128 cards. Rankings are as in standard Bezique (page 72).

The deal: Nine cards are dealt to each player, in groups of three. There is no turn-up for trumps. They are established by the first marriage declared, which thus becomes a royal marriage.

The play: This is identical to standard Bezique (page 72), except that the last trick scores fifty points, and there are the following additional declarations:

1 *Carte blanche* – if a player is dealt a hand containing no court cards, he can claim fifty points, but must show his hand to his opponent. If he then picks another non-court card, he can claim another fifty points, and so on until he finally does pick a court card. Carte blanche cannot be declared during a hand, it must be at the beginning.

2 *Ordinary sequence* – A, 10, K, Q, J of a plain suit, worth 150 points.

3 *Triple bezique* (QS–JD–QS–JD–QS–JD) is worth 1500 points.

4 *Quadruple bezique* (QS–JD–QS–JD–QS–JD–QS–JD); 4500 points.

Scoring: Game is a single deal. Brisques are only counted when a game is tied on declarations, or if the points scored in brisques will save a player from failing to reach 1000 points (known as *being rubiconed*). The player with the higher score gets a bonus of 500 points, and scores the difference between his and his opponent's score. If the loser is rubiconed, even after counting brisques, the winner gets an extra 1000 points.

Chinese Bezique

Chinese bezique is the six-pack version. Twelve cards are dealt to each player, trumps are established by the first marriage, as in Rubicon bezique, and there is no score for brisques.

There is a carte blanche declaration worth 250 points, and the following special declarations in the trump suit only:

1 Four Jacks – 400 points
2 Four Queens – 600 points
3 Four Kings – 800 points
4 Four 10s – 900 points
5 Four Aces – 1000 points

The cards used in a bezique vary according to which suit is trumps:

Trumps	Cards comprising bezique
hearts	QH and JC
diamonds	QD and JS
spades	QS and JD
clubs	QC and JH

Play is exactly the same as in Rubicon bezique (page 77), but with the last trick worth 250 points. Scoring is also the same, with game decided over a single deal, but with the winning bonus doubled up to 1000 points, and the rubiconed penalty trebled to 3000.

An **eight-deck Bezique** is also played, but each additional deck makes things more complicated, and increases the time required to play the game. I would suggest you stick at six!

Pinochle

Pinochle is the American version of Bezique. Until the emergence of Gin rummy in the middle of the twentieth century, Pinochle was the most popular two-player game in the United States.

Number of players: Two.

Cards: Two 24-card packs are used, containing nothing below a 9. The cards are ranked: Ace (highest), 10, K, Q, J, 9 (lowest). They also have values, eleven for the Ace, ten for the 10, four for the King, three for the Queen and two for the Jack. The 9 is worth nothing.

Objective: To score points for making scoring combinations, and taking tricks containing certain cards.

The deal: Each player is dealt twelve cards. The remainder of the pack forms a stock pile, the top card of which is turned up to set trumps.

The play: As in Bezique, there are two phases.

Phase one: The play is identical to Bezique (page 72); a player can play any card to a trick, then the winner can claim points for any scoring combination made. Finally, each player restores his hand to twelve cards, the winner taking the top card from stock, the loser taking the second.

As in Bezique, only one scoring combination, referred to as a *meld*, can be claimed for in a turn. Cards already used in melds can be reused to form others, provided at least one card is added from the player's hand, and the new meld is of a different class to the first.

The classes of melds are as follows:

Class A:	Sequence	A, 10, K, Q, J of trumps	150 pts
	Royal marriage	K–Q of trumps	40 pts
	Marriage	K–Q of a plain suit	20 pts
Class B:	Pinochle	QS and JD	40 pts
Class C:	Four Aces	four different suits	100 pts
	Four Kings	four different suits	80 pts
	Four Queens	four different suits	60 pts
	Four Jacks	four different suits	40 pts

The first phase ends when the stock is exhausted.

Phase two: Again, the rules for play are the same as for Bezique, with each player recovering his cards from the table and playing out, following suit where possible, and always winning a trick if a card is held which can win it.

The Dix: The 9 of trumps is known as the *dix*; there are two dixes in each hand. If one is turned up to set trumps, the dealer scores ten points. Otherwise, a player can, when it is his turn to play, declare the dix. He places it on the table, and scores ten points. The first dix to appear is then exchanged for the turned-up card.

Scoring: The points for melds are scored as they are claimed. The points for tricks are scored according to the card values, with figures rounded to multiples of ten. Only seven, eight and nine are rounded up.

Game is played up to 1000 points.

Auction Pinochle

This is a variation in which players bid for how many points they expect to score, with gambling chips changing hands according to the outcome. It is unusual in that three, rather than two players take part.

Number of players: Three.

Cards: Two 24-card packs, ranked and valued as in standard Pinochle.

The deal: Each player is dealt fifteen cards, in groups of three. The remaining three form an extra hand, a widow.

The bidding: Each player in turn may bid or pass. The player bids the number of points he expects to make on the hand, starting from a minimum of 300, and rising in multiples of at least ten.

A player cannot bid having previously passed.

The bidding ends when two players in succession pass, with the highest bidder becoming declarer.

Melding: Only the declarer melds. He adds the widow to his own hand, then lays down and scores melds as in the standard game, after having named the trump suit.

He can claim an extra ten points for each dix held.

The play: The declarer discards three cards from those still held in his hand, then picks up the cards melded on the table. He then leads to the first trick, with the normal phase two rules applying.

Once all the cards have been played, the declarer adds up his points for tricks and adds these to the points scored for melds.

Settlement: The declarer either collects or pays out to the other players, according to whether or not he has succeeded in fulfilling or exceeding his bid. The following table gives a range of standard settlements:

Bid	Number of chips
300–340	3
350–390	5
400–440	10
450–490	15
500–540	20
550–590	25
600+	30

All these amounts are doubled if spades are trumps.

Kalabriasz

Along with Bezique and Pinochle, this is the third main game in the family, and probably the most interesting. It is also known as **Klaberjass**, **Clab** and **Clobber**.

Number of players: Two.

Cards: A 32-card pack is used, with all cards below 7 stripped out.

In the trump suit the cards are ranked Jack (high), 9, A, 10, K, Q, 8, 7 (low).

In the plain suits the cards are ranked Ace (high), 10, K, Q, J, 9, 8, 7 (low).

Certain cards are valued, for scoring in tricks taken:

Jack of trumps (*jasz*)	20 points
Nine of trumps (*menel*)	14 points
Any Ace	11 points
Any 10	10 points
Any King	4 points
Any Queen	3 points
Any Jack (other than jasz)	2 points

Objective: To score points by making sequences and winning the above cards in tricks.

The deal: Six cards are dealt to each player, in groups of three. The remainder is stock, the top card of which is turned up to set the prospective trump suit.

The bidding: The non-dealer starts the bidding. He has three options:

1 Accept – the turned-up card becomes trumps, and play commences.

2 Schmeiss – this is a proposal for a new deal; the dealer must either accept the proposal, or accept the trump suit designated by the upturned card, in which case play commences.

3 *Pass* – the onus of bidding is now passed to the dealer. Again, there are three possible courses:

(a) The dealer can accept the upturned trump.

(b) The dealer can bid schmeiss, in which case the non-dealer must agree to a redeal or accept the upturned trump.

(c) The dealer can pass. The non-dealer now has the choice of nominating any suit as trumps. Alternatively, he can pass, in which case the dealer can nominate trumps. If both players pass a second time, a redeal takes place.

The player who has accepted the upturned card, or nominated the trumps, is called the *maker*.

Second deal: Once trumps have been established, three more cards are dealt to each player. The bottom card from stock is now turned up, and if trumps have been decided according to the upturned card, and the bottom card is also a trump, then if either player holds the seven of trumps (the *dix*) he can exchange it for the original upturned card.

Sequences: Before play commences, points can be scored for declaring sequences.

Sequences must contain cards of the same suit, and the ranking, for this stage only, is Ace (high), K, Q, J, 10, 9, 8, 7 (low).

A sequence of three cards is worth twenty points. A sequence of four or more cards is worth fifty.

The players must first announce the values of their best sequences. If one is higher than the other, the player with the higher sequence is awarded the number of points that the sequence is worth.

If both sequences are of the same value, the following rules apply in determining which sequence wins:

1 The sequence headed by the highest card wins.
2 If both sequences are headed by cards of the same rank, a sequence in the trump suit wins.
3 If both sequences are headed by cards of the same rank, and neither is in trumps, then no sequence points are awarded.

Note that the winning sequence could have fewer cards in it. For example, a sequence of K, Q, J, 10 would beat a sequence of Q, J, 10, 9, 8, 7.

There is a standard procedure for determining the winning sequence.

If, after announcing the values of their best sequences there is a tie, the dealer asks the non-dealer 'How high?' The non-dealer states the highest card in the sequence, at which point the dealer knows which sequence is higher.

The player with the winning sequence must show it to his opponent. In the case of a tie, both players must show their sequences.

In all cases, only the player holding the winning sequence receives the value of it, plus the value of any other sequences which he has not declared.

The play: The non-dealer leads to the first trick; thereafter the rules for play are identical to the second phase of Bezique.

If a player holds the King and Queen of trumps, known as *bella*, he can claim twenty points when the second of the two cards is played.

The scoring: The player winning the last trick scores ten points. The values of cards taken in tricks are then added up, and this is added to the sequence points for the player who had declared the highest sequence.

Having determined the final points total, the score on the hand is worked out as follows:

1 If the maker has scored more points, he receives the points difference between his score and his opponent's.
2 If the maker has scored fewer points, his opponent receives the points scored by both players. This is known as *going bate*.
3 If the players have scored the same number of points, the non-maker receives only his own points (*half bate*).

A game is played up to 500 points.

Cribbage

Cribbage is a very old English game, reputedly invented by the seventeenth-century poet and playwright Sir John Suckling. From all accounts Sir John was quite a character. He was a Member of Parliament, a well-known figure at court, a famous soldier and allegedly the finest card player in Europe. He led an eventful life and met a dramatic end. He was discovered plotting to rescue a friend from the Tower of London, fled to France and died after taking poison. He was thirty-two years old.

It is hard to imagine him finding time to invent a game as compelling as Cribbage. It is more likely that he refined an earlier game, Noddy, then took the credit for its invention.

The game has hardly changed in the past 350 years. Moreover, it is still played using a wooden board and pegs for scoring, a factor which gives Cribbage a certain rustic charm.

The most commonly played form of Cribbage nowadays is the six-card version for two players, although it can be played with fewer cards and more players.

♥ ♣ ♦ ♠

Cribbage

Number of players: Two.

Cards: One normal pack is used. The Ace scores as one, all the court cards (Kings, Queens and Jacks) score ten. Other cards are counted at face value.

Objective: To reach 121 points, the score being kept on a cribbage board.

The deal: Six cards are dealt to each player, and the remainder of the pack is placed face-down alongside. The deal alternates between the players.

Discarding: Both players must discard two cards, face down. The four cards thus discarded form a third hand, known as *the crib*. The contents of the crib belong to the dealer, but remain hidden until the end of the hand. In deciding which cards to part with, the players must consider the scoring possibilities of their hands. There are two phases of scoring, the *play* and the *show*.

The scoring combinations within the players' hands and the crib are counted up at the show phase, so these must be the main consideration when making the decision.

Scoring combinations:

1   *A pair* – two points.
2   *A pair royal* – three cards of the same rank – six points.
3   *A double pair royal* – four cards of the same rank – twelve points.
4   *A sequence* of at least three cards; they need not be the same suit – one point for each card.
5   *A flush* – all cards of the same suit – one point for each card.
6   *Fifteen* – any combination of cards which adds up to 15 – two points.

The cut: After both players have discarded, the non-dealer cuts the deck and the dealer turns up the top card from the bottom section. This card is known as the *start*, and is used in the show phase. If it is a Jack, the dealer scores two points.

The play: Starting with the non-dealer, both players must, in turn, lay down their four cards, one at a time. The cards are placed face-up, a separate pile in front of each player. As each card is placed, the players must call out the cumulative total, and any points scored. Points are scored whenever pairs, pairs royal, double pairs royal, sequences or fifteens are formed during play. Note that flushes are not scored during play.

A sequence of cards can score regardless of the order in which the cards were played. For example, if the order of cards played was 2,5,4,3 the player contributing the 3 would score four points for a four-card sequence. If his opponent held an Ace or a 6, he could play it and extend the sequence to five cards, scoring five points.

The cumulative total cannot go beyond thirty-one. If a player cannot play without going beyond thirty-one, he says 'go' and his opponent continues to play any cards which will keep the total within the limit. If thirty-one is reached exactly, the player who has placed the last card scores two points. If the score is below thirty-one and neither player can go, the player who has placed the last card scores one point. Play then restarts at zero.

The last player to place a card scores 'one for last'.

All points scored during play are pegged immediately. It is quite legitimate for a player to win the game part way through a hand.

The show: The non-dealer shows first – obviously if he is very near the end this can be sufficient to bring him victory. He counts up his scoring combinations, including in his calculations the start card turned up. If he holds the Jack of the suit turned up, he scores one point. If he holds a four-card flush in his hand, and the start is the same suit, he scores five points.

When the non-dealer has finished counting up and pegging out, the same procedure is carried out by the dealer. Having counted up his own hand, the dealer counts up the crib in exactly the same way.

Strategy: The first decision involves discarding. With experience, it soon becomes obvious which combinations are good ones to keep. You should always remember whose crib you are discarding to. If it is your own, try to discard two cards which combine well together, although not if this reduces the potential in your own hand. If it is your opponent's crib, try to find unhelpful discards.

When leading in the play phase, it is best to play a low card – this will prevent your opponent having the opportunity of an immediate fifteen. A 4 is probably best. Avoid bringing the total up to twenty-one, as there is always a fair chance that your opponent will have a court card in his hand, thus enabling him to score two for thirty-one.

The current state of the score should be a consideration. If you are almost home, it may be worth keeping cards which are likely to be useful in the play, even if this means sacrificing show points. Aces can be very helpful, particularly as the total approaches thirty-one.

At first sight, counting up hands in Cribbage may appear somewhat complicated, and it is probably the case that in your first few games you may miss the odd fifteen here and there, or the occasional sequence in play. However, it will soon become easier. Perhaps these two small sample hands will help.

Sample Hand – Cribbage

The two players are Agatha and Basil.

Agatha deals the first hand, and the cards are as follows:

Agatha	Basil
Spades 6	Spades Q, 10
Hearts J, 6, 4	Hearts Q
Diamonds 2	Diamonds 8, 3
Clubs 5	Clubs Q

Agatha has a very useful hand. At first sight, it might seem sensible to keep the two 6s, plus the Jack and 5 which add up to fifteen. But look more closely. There are two sequences, 4, 5, 6 twice, one for each 6; moreover, each sequence adds up to fifteen $(4 + 5 + 6)$. Therefore, regardless of what card is turned up, the hand is worth at least twelve points: six for two sequences, four for two

fifteens, and two for the pair of 6s. Agatha discards JH and 2D, keeping 6S, 6H, 4H and 5C.

Basil's decision is more clear cut. He will keep the three Queens – but which other card? He could keep 10S, because if a Jack was turned up this would give him three three-card sequences. Alternatively, he could keep 3D, which is likely to be more useful in the play, and which would combine with a 2 to form three fifteens, should a 2 be turned up. He decides to keep 10S, discarding 8D and 3D.

The pack is cut, and 3H is turned up.

The play

Basil leads QS – total 10.
Agatha plays 5C – total 15, scoring 2 points.
Basil plays QH – total 25.
Agatha plays 6S – total 31, scoring 2 points.
Basic restarts with QC – total 10.
Agatha plays 6H – total 16.
Basil plays 10S – total 26.
Agatha plays 4H – total 30, scoring 1 point.

So after the play Agatha leads by 5–0.

The show: Basil counts up first. The 3H turned up hasn't helped him at all. All he scores is six points for his pair royal.

Agatha has done well. The 3H has extended her three-card sequences to four-card sequences; also, notice that another fifteen has appeared: The two 6s plus the 3H. Altogether Agatha has scored sixteen points: eight for sequences, six for fifteens and two for a pair.

Agatha now counts up the crib, which comprises JH, 8D, 3D and 2D. Along with 3H, Agatha can see two fifteens and a pair. Ah, and there is also the extra point for holding the Jack of the suit turned up, often known as *one for his nob*. Total 7 points.

Running total: Agatha 28   Basil 6.

Basil deals the second hand as follows:

Basil		Agatha	
Spades	3, A	Spades	10, 5
Hearts	3	Hearts	K
Diamonds	8, 7, 2	Diamonds	6, A
Clubs	–	Clubs	8

Basil has an easy choice, since it is his crib. He can discard 8D and 7D, thus keeping two sequences and a pair, while at the same time giving himself something to look forward to when he counts up the crib.

Agatha has a fairly moderate hand, two fifteens but nothing much else. She decides to keep 6D, along with 10S, 5S and KH, in the hope that a 4 or 7 is turned up to give her a sequence. She discards AD and 8C.

The pack is cut, and AC turned up.

The play

    Agatha leads 10S – total 10.

    Basil plays 3S – total 13.

    Agatha plays KH – total 23.

    Basil plays 2D – total 25 (note that he avoided playing 3H, which would have given her 31).

    This would have brought the total to 26, and judging by the cards Agatha has played, there is a strong chance that she has a five.

    Agatha plays 5S – total 30.

    Basil plays AS – total 31, scoring 2 points.

    Agatha restarts with 6D – total 6.

    Basil plays 3H – total 9, scoring 1 point for last.

The show: Agatha counts up first. AC is no help, so she scores only four points, two for each fifteen.

    Basil has been more fortunate. The AC has converted his two sequences into four, to be precise: AS, 2D, 3S; AS, 2D, 3H; AC, 2D, 3S; AC, 2D, 3H. Each is worth three points. There are also two pairs: Aces and 3s. Total sixteen points.

    He now turns to the crib, which comprises 8D, 7D, AD and 8C. Each of the 8/7 combinations adds up to fifteen, and there are also two pairs. Total eight points.

Running total: Agatha 32   Basil 33.

    The two hands illustrate one of the joys of Cribbage. Things can turn round very dramatically.

If you find the scoring difficult in six-card Cribbage, then avoid the seven-card version! It is played up to 181 points. Seven cards are dealt, with two discarded. Otherwise the rules are identical. The problem lies in seeing all the fifteens and sequences concealing themselves amidst seven cards, rather than six.

Five-card cribbage is rather easier. Five cards are dealt to each player, with two discarded. Therefore the crib has four cards, while the players' hands have only three. Again, scoring and play is identical to the six-card version.

    Although Cribbage is primarily a two-player game, there is a three-handed version. Each player is dealt five cards, of which one is discarded. An additional card is dealt to the crib. Play begins with the player to the left of the dealer, then moves in a clockwise direction. The show goes in the same order as the play.

A Cribbage board.

Gambling

Everyone gambles. In its broadest sense, gambling simply means taking a risk in the hope of gaining something. So we continually gamble throughout our lives. When we take a job, we are gambling that it proves to be the right one, with the best prospects. The Wednesday night bingo session is gambling. 'Investing' in the stock market is gambling. Even buying tickets for the church raffle is a gamble.

But the true gambler is something different. He is the man who bets big money, with the risk of losing the lot. He strives for thrills and excitement, dreams of fame and fortune, and risks poverty and destitution.

Freud saw gambling as a sexual substitute. Others see it as a revolt against boredom. The cynical view is that gambling is the one sure way of getting nothing for something.

The History of Gambling

Gamblers are not a new species. Dice have been found in the tombs of the pharaohs in Egypt, and betting on the chariot races in ancient Rome was as commonplace as nipping into the local bookie's to put some money on the 2.30 at the local races.

Cards became gambling tools relatively recently, late in the fourteenth century. But they soon caught on. Henry VIII was a notorious card-player and gambler, described at the time as 'a gamester of the most unscrupulous sort'. Despite his own enthusiasm, the King actually banned card playing, except at Christmas.

A more formal suppression of gambling was imposed in Cromwell's time, and remained for over three hundred years.

The situation was similar in America. For many years gambling was illegal, and illicit card schools were formed, which continuously struggled to stay clear of the law. The most famous ones were on the Mississippi steamboats in the nineteenth century. The best-equipped vessels were floating casinos, with slot machines, dice games and numerous card tables. Many of the games we play today are said to have been invented on the Mississippi.

Nowadays there is a more liberal attitude to gambling. In Britain almost any kind of bet is possible, any time, anywhere. You could even bet on whether the Loch Ness monster exists, although you might have to wait a while before finding out whether you had won or lost. In America the laws vary from state to state. Nevada has always been at the forefront of gambling in the United States, hence the emergence of cities such as Las Vegas.

The Mathematics of Gambling

Assuming that the cards are not fixed, and that the players are honest, law-abiding types, gambling with cards boils down to a question of mathematics. This is not to say that you need to be a mathematical genius to win money at cards, or that a mathematical genius will automatically win. But it is helpful to have some understanding of the principles involved, the laws of probabilities and averages, and the percentages which guarantee that a casino does not lose money.

The Law of Probability and the Law of Averages

With cards, it is always possible to calculate the odds on a particular event occurring. For example, if you are playing poker and have been dealt three Aces (lucky you!), the chance of getting a fourth if you change two cards must be 2 in 47 (1 in 23.5). This is because there are forty-seven cards that you cannot see, two of which you will be receiving. This is an illustration of the law of probability, which states that:

> The probability of any particular outcome to an event (provided that all outcomes are equally likely) is the proportion between the number of cases favourable to that outcome, and the total number of cases possible.

The law of probability always applies. Calculating the probability is the difficult part! Great minds from the past have struggled with the problem.

Galileo and Pascal were two early pioneers. Nowadays computers make the whole thing much easier, but be warned: if you are seen carrying any electronic calculating device into a casino, you will be politely but firmly asked to leave.

The law of averages is totally different. It is also known as 'the gambler's fallacy' – and that just about sums it up. The law of averages proposes that if an outcome has occurred a number of times, it cannot continue to do so.

Players argue that if they have been losing heavily, their luck must be about to change. Unfortunately this ignores the second fundamental law of gambling, the principle of independent events. It states that:

Each and every chance event occurs independently, without any relation to previous events.

For example, assume that you have tossed a coin ten times, and each time it has come up heads. If you toss it again, the chance of it coming up heads is exactly 50%.

The casino's percentage

If you are playing cards for money with a few friends at home, you may win or you may lose, but at the end of the day the total amount of money won and lost will cancel out. For the management of a casino this is not good enough. If they are to run a card game, they must make money out of it. This can be done in one of two ways:

1 *Straight percentage* – players' winnings are 'taxed' by the casino with, say, five per cent being deducted. An example of a game with percentage takings is Chemin de Fer.

2 *Within the game* – in certain games the rules ensure that the casino makes a certain percentage, by forcing the players to take actions which actually work slightly against them. Examples of such games are Blackjack and Baccarat.

Here are some popular casino games, and the estimated percentages which the casino expects to make. The lower the percentage, the better your chance!

Game	Casino's percentage per hand
Blackjack	5.9
Baccarat	1.34
Trente et quarante	1.5
Ziginette	3.0

Of course very few people play one hand. Over a month, and depending on the number of people playing the game, the casino might expect to make 26 per cent profits on Blackjack and 10 per cent on Baccarat.

Systems

It has always been the ambition of gamblers to turn a risk into a sure-fire investment. In theory, systems are the answer. You follow the system and rake in the winnings. But it is not quite that simple. Hundreds of thousands of hours of work have gone into devising systems, and numerous books have been printed purporting to provide the ultimate answers, yet none has been found which can guarantee success. Here are a few of the attempts:

Martingale system: This is used on even-money bets, where the return is equal to the stake. An example of a card game with even-money returns is Baccarat. Starting with a stake of one unit, the gambler doubles up every time he loses. When he eventually wins, he starts again with a stake of one.

There are two problems with the system. Firstly, the gambler must have a lot of money, to cater for a string of losses. Secondly, even if his funds are unlimited, the maximum bet in the casino is, and this prevents the gambler operating the system effectively.

D'Alembert system: This is again based on even-money chances. The gambler adds one unit to his stake after a loss, and deducts one after a win. Here the casino betting limits are less likely to come into effect, but the wins are less spectacular, and because every game has a house percentage, the gambler must eventually lose out.

Card-counting systems: These involve keeping track of which cards have appeared, and altering bets as the probabilities change. They are applicable to games such as Blackjack, and offer the gambler the best chance of long-term success. The problem is the human factor – it takes a powerful mind to work such a system, and one careless session in a casino can undo months of hard graft.

Perhaps the last word on systems should go to an anonymous casino owner who once said: 'Show me a man with a sure-fire system and plenty of hard cash to bet on it, and I'll send a taxi-cab to pick him up.'

Inscription on a tombstone in Boot Hill cemetery, Dodge City, Kansas, USA:

> 'Played five Aces
> Now playing the harp.'

'Gambling is the great leveller. All men are equal – at cards.'
Nikolai Gogol

The Big-Time Gamblers
Despite the mathematical evidence to the contrary, luck does exist, particularly over a short period; and a little luck can produce gigantic returns.

The big winners at gambling fall into two categories:
1. Those who have a run of luck, and bet high during it.
2. Those who are great card players, and who take on others less gifted than themselves for very high stakes.

The great tales of gambling at the card table feature both.

The Man Who Broke the Bank at Monte Carlo
In July 1891, a small-time gambler named Charles de Ville Wells struck such a rich vein of luck that he caused the casino at Monte Carlo to run out of cash, not once but *six* times. He was actually playing a roulette wheel, but it could equally well have been any even-money bet. Operating the Martingale system, he won more than £40,000 after arriving with less than £400.

The epilogue is that Charles de Ville Wells died penniless in 1926.

93

The Most Daring Gambler in the World
Or so said George Devol, one of the notorious nineteenth-century riverboat gamblers. He published a book of his adventures in 1892: *Forty Years a Gambler on the Mississippi*. The title page alone sounds like an autobiography, '. . . could steal cards and cheat the boys at eleven; stack a deck at fourteen; won hundreds of thousands from paymasters, cotton buyers, defaulters and thieves . . .' and so it goes on.

Certainly he lived on his wits. After fleecing his fellow passengers he would often escape in disguise, or swim ashore amidst the splash of misdirected bullets.

Anyone was fair prey to Devol, although he could display an impish sense of fun on occasion. Having tricked a clergyman out of his money, he would often return it with the comment: 'Go, and sin no more.'

Poker Alice
Alice Ivers was born in England in 1850, and had a high-class upbringing and a finishing-school education. Following her husband's death, she turned to gambling, and claimed to play poker better than any other living man or woman. She also ran a brothel, murdered a soldier, and sold illicit whisky. Yet she claimed to have high moral standards, and refused to play cards on a Sunday!

The Greek Syndicate
The greatest casino card player of all time was Nico Zographos. Along with three fellow-countrymen, he formed the Greek Syndicate, a group of gamblers who played Baccarat for enormous stakes, all round the world.

Over £1000 million passed through his hands during his career. Unlike many famous gamblers, Zographos died in 1953 a wealthy man – he left over £5 million.

One of his victims was André Citroen, the French car manufacturer, and an

inveterate but unsuccessful gambler. Eventually Citroen lost no less than 30 million francs to Zographos, and had to sell his business to pay his debts.

Nick the Greek

The best-known gambler of recent times has been a man whose career largely paralleled that of Zographos. He is Nicholas Dandolos, better known as Nick the Greek. Scrupulously honest and impeccably attired, Nick the Greek was a superb poker player, and played for enormous stakes. He was not always successful. He once lost $605,000 on a single deal, to his chief adversary Arnold Rothstein. Rothstein bought Nick a Rolls Royce out of the winnings. Nick graciously refused the gift with the comment: 'Who needs a car in New York?'

Beat the Dealer

Ed Thorp is a mathematics professor, not a gambler. But in 1961 he put forward a theory on Blackjack which actually seemed to provide a way of beating the casino. His views were expounded in his book, *Beat the Dealer*.

Thorp's system was based on card counting, and the changing odds as cards with a value of ten appeared.

With the help of two full-time gamblers, Thorp put his theory into practice. It was so successful that he received the ultimate compliment from the casino owners – they banned him from playing!

The problem with Thorp's system is that it took a professor of mathematics to invent it . . . and it takes someone similar to use it!

'True luck consists not in holding the best of cards at the table;
Luckiest he who knows just when to rise and go home.'

John Hay

Banking Games

The distinguishing feature of banking games is that they pit individuals against the establishment – usually the players against the casino.

In some cases this is the only way the game can be played. But there are others, such as Blackjack, which can equally well be played at home, with one of the players acting as banker.

Blackjack (Social)

Blackjack is the casino name for the game. It is also known as **Pontoon**, **Vingt-et-un** and **Twenty-one**. Like so many contemporary card games, its roots seem to lie in many countries and its ancestors are legion. One thing is for certain: Blackjack is now the most widely played banking game in the world, at casinos as far apart as Sydney and New York.

There are really two separate forms of the game; the social version which can be played anywhere, and the casino version. I shall deal first with the social one, then describe the differences between the two.

Number of players: Two to ten.

Cards: One normal pack is used. Each card has a value. The Ace is worth one or eleven, the court cards count ten, and all other cards are counted at face value.

Objective: To collect cards with a higher total value than the dealer's, provided this is not greater than twenty-one.

The deal: One card is dealt to each player, including the dealer, who is also referred to as the banker.

The betting: After looking at this card, each player must make a bet, which he places on the table in front of him. The banker then looks at his card, and may double if he wishes, in which case the other players must double their bets or drop out, losing their initial stake.

The banker then deals a second card to each player. If the banker finds that he has got 21, made up of an Ace and a 10 or court card (known as a *Blackjack* or a *natural*), every player must pay him double their initial stake. The hands are then thrown in. If one of the other players also held a natural, then he need pay only his stake, rather than double it.

If the banker does not hold a natural, but one of the other players does, the better wins twice his stake, and at the end of the hand he becomes the banker.

Once the naturals have been dealt with, each player must make one of the following choices:

1   *Stand* – the player chooses to stick with his hand as dealt.
2   *Twist* – the player requests another card, which is turned face up by the banker.
3   *Buy* – the player requests another card face down, and increases his stake.
4   *Split* – if a player has a pair, he can lay the two cards face up on the table. The banker deals him two more cards, one on each, then the player can twist or stand as he wishes, playing with the equivalent of two open hands.

A player can buy and twist more than once, although the following rules must be observed:

1   A player cannot buy for more than his original stake.
2   If a player has twisted for a third card, he cannot then buy a fourth. On the other hand, a player who has bought a third card can twist a fourth.
3   A player cannot hold more than five cards. If five are held, and the total is less than twenty-one, the banker must pay double (unless the banker himself has five cards, in which case the banker wins).
4   Unless he has five cards, a player cannot stand on fifteen or less – he must twist or buy.

If a player completes a twenty-one comprising three 7s, the banker must pay three times the stake.

When a player buys or twists, and the total of his cards exceeds twenty-one, he is *bust* and must hand his cards and his stake to the banker.

Eventually every player apart from the banker will have stood or gone bust. The banker then turns his cards and deals himself cards as required. If he goes bust, he pays everyone still in the game the value of their stake. Alternatively, he stands, and pays only those with a higher score. He is paid by everyone with a lower or equal score.

Strategy: Blackjack is a game of probabilities. It is generally best to stand as soon as you are in a position to. For example, if you hold a hand worth sixteen there are only five cards out of thirteen which will not cause you to go bust. Of course if you already have four cards, it may be worth the risk so as to double your winnings.

As banker, it is probably worth doubling on any card above an eight.

In the years since computers first appeared, they have frequently been put to work calculating odds at Blackjack, in an effort to 'beat the house'. Two of the earliest computerized Blackjack studies were carried out at The Atomic Energy Commission in Los Alamos, New Mexico, and at the US Army's Aberdeen Proving Ground in Maryland. So now we know what members of the armed forces do in their spare time!

Blackjack (Casino)

Blackjack as played in casinos round the world is different from social Blackjack; the variations are as follows:

The players must place bets before the deal. The two cards are then dealt out simultaneously; in some casinos they will be face up, in others face down. The dealer is an employee of the casino. His first card is always dealt face up. If it is a 10, an Ace or a court card, he will look to see whether he has a natural. If so, he collects all bets, although players holding naturals have theirs returned.

Buying is not allowed, but *doubling down* is. A player can place his cards face up, then double his stake to receive a third card, face down, which is turned up only at the end of the hand when comparisons are made with the dealer's hand.

The dealer has no decisions to make. He must twist on sixteen and stand on seventeen. On tied hands the players' bets are returned.

Sample Hand – Blackjack

The five players are five typical gamblers. Timid Tim, who would not believe he could win even if he was the only player; Reckless Ruth, who'll bet on anything, any time; Positive Pete, who knows he is better than anyone else, and relishes the chance to prove it; Stupid Sam, who has just learnt that there are four suits in a pack of cards; and Mathematical Moira, who always knows the odds, but not necessarily how to apply them.

First round

Tim cuts the cards and becomes the banker. He then deals everyone their first card.

Ruth – 4D; not a good card, but that doesn't stop Ruth. She bets three chips.

Pete – 5S; 5 is the worst card in Blackjack, because the most likely value of the next card is ten, and this would give him a total of 15. He would not be able to stand, and the chances of going bust on the following card are quite high. Pete appreciates this fact, and bets only one chip.

Sam – JD; any court card is promising, even Sam knows that. He bets two chips.

Moira – 6D; not too good, she bets one chip.

Tim's own card is 8S. He decides not to double.

Second round

Tim deals a second round of cards, KD to Ruth, 2H to Pete, 6D to Sam, AC to Moira and 6S to himself.

Ruth now has 4D, KD; total fourteen. She has no choice but to twist. Tim hands her KC, she announces that she is bust, and hands over her cards and her chips.

Pete now has 5S, 2H, total seven. He decides to buy, but can pay only one chip, since that was his initial stake. He gets AS. He could now count his hand as eighteen (2 + 5 + 11), but he has greater plans. He buys another card, 5D, then another, 3D. He now has a five-card hand, worth sixteen, and a total of four chips staked.

Sam now has JD, 6D; total sixteen. He could, and probably should, stand. But not Sam. He twists, receives 9C and hands over his stake.

Moira now has 6D, AC; total seventeen or seven. She decides to stand.

Tim has 8S, 6S; total fourteen. With a sinking heart, he turns over the top card. It turns out to be 4S. He now has eighteen, and stands.

There are only two players left in apart from Tim; Pete with his five-card sixteen, and Moira with seventeen.

Settlement

Although Pete's score is lower than Tim's, he has a five-card hand. This wins automatically, and is paid double the amount staked. Since he has staked four chips, he is paid eight.

Tim's eighteen beats Moira's seventeen, so he receives her one chip.

Overall only Pete has done well. Tim has won six but lost eight, whereas all the others have lost their stakes.

When you're having a bad day on the Blackjack table, it might seem that it is virtually impossible to get cards to total twenty-one. Not quite true. In fact, in a normal pack, there are 171,060 different combinations of cards which will total twenty-one!

Baccarat

Baccarat, along with its close cousin Chemin de fer (often anglicized as *Chemmy*), is one of the more popular banking games. Its attraction is difficult to understand. There is no skill involved, indeed there are no decisions whatsoever to take regarding the cards themselves – only the nature of the bet is in the hands of the players.

   Yet there is a certain aura about the game: the massive card deck used and its special dealing box (the *shoe*); the wooden palette on which the cards are distributed; and the customary formal dress of the players as they sit around an enormous baize table.

Number of players: Up to twelve, although only two hands are dealt, one to the players and one to the bank. The table will look something like this:

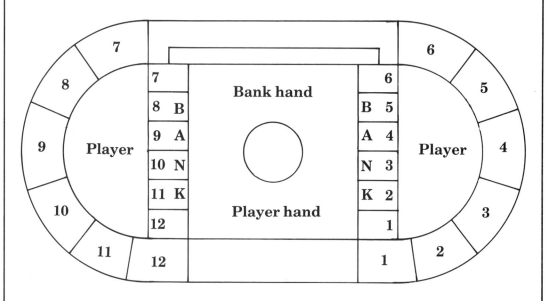

Cards: Six or eight packs are shuffled together. Each card has a value: Ace is one, court cards ten, and all others face value.

The deal: Two cards are dealt to the player hand, and two to the bank hand. Players have the choice of betting on either.

Objective: To get a hand comprising two or three cards, in which the total is as near to nine as possible. For hands totalling more than nine, only the units are counted. For example, a 7 and a 9 (total sixteen) would count as six.

The betting: Each player places a bet, any amount between the casino's minimum and maximum limits, on either the bank's hand or the players' hand to win.

The play: The banker and one of the players look at their respective hands. If either has a hand totalling eight or nine (a *natural*), it is turned up and bets are settled. If both have naturals, the higher wins. If they are the same, no money changes hands.

Assuming neither has a natural, the player and the banker must draw or stand according to strict rules. The rules for the player are simple:

1　If the hand is worth between nought and five, the player must draw a card.
2　If the hand is worth six or seven, the player must stand.

　If the player draws, the banker deals him an extra card, face up.

　The actions of the banker vary according to the rank of the card dealt to the player. They are as follows:

Value held	Banker must draw after dealing . . .	Banker must stand after dealing . . .
0, 1, 2	any card	–
3	A, 2, 3, 4, 5, 6, 7, 9, 10	8
4	2, 3, 4, 5, 6, 7	A, 8, 9, 10
5	4, 5, 6, 7	A, 2, 3, 8, 9, 10
6	6, 7	A, 2, 3, 4, 5, 8, 9, 10
7	–	any card

Settling bets:　If the players' hand wins, the bank pays out the amount bet, an even-money return. If the bank's hand wins, the bank pays even, but takes a five per cent cut from the winnings.

Chemin De Fer

The main difference between this game and Baccarat is that the bank in Chemin de fer is not fixed; each player in turn has the opportunity to become banker. Theoretically it could be played at home, although it might have to be without the familiar table and trimmings!

The choice of first banker can be by auction, with players bidding for it, by cut or by prior agreement.

Everyone must bet against the bank.

Where Chemin de fer is played in casinos, a croupier is in attendance. He shuffles the cards, supervises the cut, and discards (*burns*) the top three cards, to ensure that no fixing of the deck has occurred. He also keeps a check on the winnings made as banker by each player, because the casino takes a five per cent cut of all bank winnings.

The betting: This takes place before the deal. The banker specifies an amount which he is prepared to put up, then the players place bets totalling anything up to, but not above, the banker's specified amount. A single player can bet against the entire bank by calling *Banco* – in this case all the other bets are void.

The deal: The banker deals two cards to himself, and two cards to the table, as the players' hand.

The play: Essentially this is the same as Baccarat, except that both the player and the banker are given a little more flexibility. The player can stand on five, whilst the banker can draw or stand if he has three, and he has just dealt a 9.

The settlement: If the bank wins, it collects the players' bets. If it loses, it pays out the amount bet. At the end of the session, the casino collects five per cent of each player's winnings as banker.

Passing the bank: If the banker has lost a hand, he must pass on the bank to the next player at the table.

Although the casino cannot lose at Chemin de fer, Baccarat is now more popular because only one player is needed to start a game.

102

Banking card games are a fluctuating species. New ones emerge, and old ones die out. This can be explained partly in terms of changing tastes, but sometimes there are more sinister reasons. Certain games leave themselves open to the chicanery of unscrupulous casino owners. And if people realize that they are being duped, they will soon turn to other forms of gambling.

Two such examples are **Chinese Fan Tan**, which was very popular in the Wild West, and **Faro**, which is still found in a few Las Vegas casinos, but has largely died out.

Chinese Fan Tan
Number of players: Any number.
Cards: One normal pack is used.
The betting: The players can bet on an outcome of 1, 2, 3 or 4. These are designated as the four corners of a playing card, usually a Joker, which is placed face up in the centre of the table. Each player places his chips at the appropriate corner. It is possible to bet on two numbers, by placing the chips between two corners. In the diagram, Bet one is for an outcome of 2; Bet two is for an outcome of 1 or 4.

Bet one

Bet two

The play: One of the players shuffles the deck, then the banker, an employee of the casino, cuts it, removing a large portion of the pack. This he then deals out in groups of four. The remainder is the number paid out on. If the cards deal out precisely, the winning number is 4.

It is easy to see how the game could become crooked, either through careful cutting, or dishonest dealing.

Faro

Faro has an interesting background, first coming to prominence in the court of Louis XIV. It made its way to America and the infamous gambling havens of the Mississippi steamboats. It then reached dry land where playing Faro became known as *bucking the tiger*, because, with gambling illegal, the presence of a Faro game was indicated by hanging a sign showing a tiger outside the illicit establishment.

Number of players: Up to ten.

Cards: One normal pack is used.

Additional requirements: As well as betting chips, special Faro *coppers* are needed. These are hexagonal chips which, when placed on top of normal chips, convert a bet to win into a bet to lose. A *casekeeper* is also needed. This is an apparatus like an abacus which shows which cards have so far appeared. Finally, a special Faro table is required, on which the bets are placed. It has thirteen cards fixed to it, representing the thirteen different ranks:

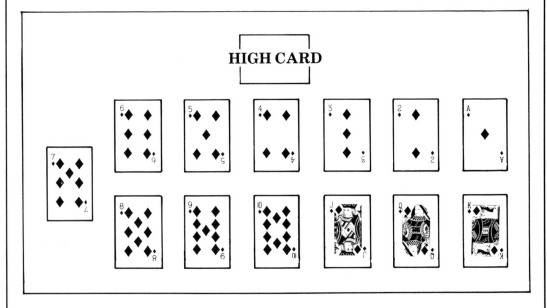

The play: The shuffled cards are placed in a dealing box, face up. Betting takes place (see below), then the top card, known as the *soda* is removed. The next card is then placed on a discard pile, and the new top card wins. Thereafter each round, which is preceded by betting, takes the following form:

1 The previous winning card is removed.
2 The next card loses, and is placed on the discard pile.
3 The new top card wins, and all bets are settled.

As each card appears, it is registered on the casekeeper, so that the players know what is yet to come.

The pack of cards and the casekeeper are controlled by employees of the gambling establishment.

The betting: Through the course of the game there are three possible bets:

1 ***Bets on one number*** – the better wins if that number comes up; the bet is made by a better putting his chips on the appropriate card on the Faro table.

2 ***Bets on a set of numbers*** – as above, but the chips are placed between the appropriate numbers.

3 ***Bets taking action through the game*** – these are bets which are placed at the beginning of the game, and win or lose on each turn. If the bet wins, the better is paid the amount of his initial stake. If it loses, he must pay the amount of the stake. The stake itself remains throughout the game. There are two types of bet:

  (i) *High* – the winning card on a turn is higher than the losing card.

  (ii) *Odd or even* – if a player has bet even, he wins if the winning card on a turn is even, vice versa if the bet is odd.

Any bet can be 'turned round' into a bet on the losing card, rather than the winning card. This is done by placing one of the coppers on top of the betting chips, known as *coppering the bet*.

The last turn: The game continues normally until only three cards remain, then a special series of bets comes into operation. The casekeeper shows exactly which three cards are left. The possible bets are:

1 ***Normal win or lose***, ignoring the last card which is known as the *hock*.

2 ***Calling the Turn*** – predicting the precise order of the three cards. This applies if they are of three different ranks.

3 ***Cat Hop bet*** – the same as calling the turn, but where two cards are the same rank.

Settlement: Calling the Turn is paid at 4 to 1; a successful Cat Hop is paid 2 to 1; all other bets are paid at evens. If one bet has covered both winning and losing cards, the better neither wins nor loses money.

As in Chinese Fan Tan, a crooked dealer can easily rig the pack.

105

During the eighteenth century, Brook's club had to have a large semi-circular section cut out of its Faro table, to accommodate the enormous stomach of Charles James Fox, one of its best customers.

Some of the early banking games have survived, but in a much limited sphere. Two examples are **Lottery** and **Red dog**.

Lottery

This is rarely played in casinos, but can be fun with friends.

Number of players: Any number.

Cards: Two normal packs are used, but are kept separate.

The betting: Before the deal, each player must put an agreed number of chips into a pot.

The deal: Each player is dealt one card, face down, from the first pack. The second pack is then taken, and a second card is dealt to each player, this time face up. (Each player deals in turn.)

The play: Players can stake additional bets on their face-up cards, then each player looks at his down-card. If any player can match his down-card in rank with any of the face-up cards, he wins the pot. If more than one player finds a match, the pot is divided.

If a player can match in colour as well as rank, he receives one chip from the player whose face-up card has given him the match.

If a player matches with his own face-up card, he collects his own stake, any other stakes on cards of the same rank, plus one chip from each player in the game.

Any stakes which are not collected in this way remain for the next deal.

Red Dog

The army is a fertile breeding ground for gambling games, particularly those where nothing is needed apart from a pack of cards and a little cash. Red dog was a favourite during World War II; fast and exciting, but easily abandoned if the call to combat duty came through.

Number of players: Two to eight.

Cards: One normal pack is used.

First round of betting: Each player must place an agreed stake into a pot before the deal.

Objective: To hold in your hand a card in the same suit but higher in rank than a card dealt by the dealer.

The deal: Four cards are dealt to each player. (Each player deals in turn.)

Second round of betting: After looking at their cards, each player must place a bet or drop out. The level of the bet must be at least as high as the initial stake, but not greater than the total amount of the pot.

The play: Once all bets have been placed, the dealer gives the top card from the pack to the first player. If the player holds a higher card in the same suit, he wins, and is paid from the pot an equivalent amount to his stake on the second round of betting. If the player loses, his stake is added to the pot.

This procedure is carried out for each active player, including the dealer.

Any money remaining in the pot stays there for the next hand, although at any stage the players can agree to divide the pot, if it looks as though it may be becoming too big.

If the pot runs out, a player can be owed money, and paid back once the pot is replenished.

Different areas of the world have different favourite banking games. Blackjack and Baccarat are very much American. On the continent of Europe, two of the best-loved games are **Trente et quarante** and **Ziginette**.

107

Trente et Quarante

Trente et quarante is also known as **Rouge et noir**, and together its two names encapsulate the game; the winning total is between thirty and forty, on the red or black row.

Number of players: Any number.

Cards: Six packs are used, shuffled together. Each card has a value. Ace is one, court cards are ten, and all other cards take their face values.

Additional requirement: Trente et quarante has a special table, on which cards are dealt and bets are placed. It is a double table, each half of which looks like this:

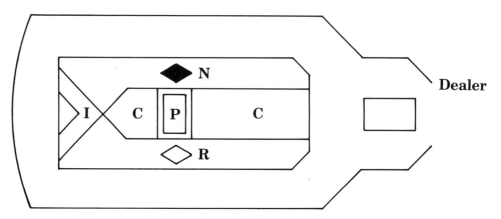

Objective: To bet which of two rows has cards dealt to it totalling a points value nearer thirty-one.

The play: After the pack has been shuffled and cut, and players have placed bets (see below), the dealer, an employee of the casino, places cards, face up, on the black row, announcing the total as he goes along. As soon as the total exceeds thirty, the dealer starts placing cards in a similar way on the red row. Once this total exceeds thirty, the two totals on the black and red rows are compared, with the row comprising the lower total winning.

The betting: The following bets are available to the players:

1 *Red or black to win* – chips are placed on the area marked R or N (*rouge* or *noir*).

2 *The colour of the first card turned up will match the eventual winning row* – chips are placed on one of the areas marked C (*couleur*).

3 *The colour of the first card turned up will match the eventual losing row* – chips are placed on the area marked I (*inverse*).

Settlement of bets: All winning bets are paid at evens. But of course the casino must take its percentage. This is done where the row totals are tied. If the totals are greater than thirty-one, bets are returned in full. However, if the totals are exactly thirty-one, the bank returns only half the stake; alternatively, the player can put his bet *in prison*, the area marked P on the table. If the bet then wins, the stake is returned. If it loses, the bank takes the whole of the stake.

Ziginette

This is the main banking game in Italy. It is also widely played in the United States by Americans of Italian descent.

Number of players: Two or more, of which one is the dealer, or banker.

Cards: A 40-card pack is used, with the 8s, 9s and 10s stripped out.

The deal: A dealing box is used, from which two cards are dealt face up to the table. This exposes a third card, the banker's card.

The betting: The players place their bets on the cards dealt to the table. In essence, they are predicting that the card on which they bet will not be matched before the banker's card is matched. A match occurs when a new card appears which is of the same rank as one of the cards already exposed.

The play: Once all bets have been placed, the banker removes his card from the dealing box, and places it under the rest of the pack, but protruding so that most of it is still visible. This exposes the top card of the pack. If it matches one of the table cards, the banker collects all the money bet on that card. If it matches the banker's card, he pays out to each of the players the amount they have staked.

If there are no matches, the exposed card becomes a table card and can have bets placed on it. The next card in the pack is then exposed, and the settlement process takes place once more.

The hand ends only when the banker's card has been matched.

If cards appear which have already been matched at an earlier stage, they are *dead*, and are removed from the dealing box.

If a match occurs in the opening deal, the pack is reshuffled and the hand is redealt. This is known as a *No deal*.

Settling bets: All bets are settled during the course of play, or when the banker's card is matched.

If Ziginette is played in a casino, ten per cent of all winnings made as banker are taken by the house. A croupier must be in attendance throughout, to maintain a record of these winnings.

Monte Bank

Monte has an unenviable reputation. It has long been the main game in illegal gambling establishments, and has invariably attracted hustlers and cheats like bees to a honeypot.

There are many versions of Monte. This is one of the simpler ones.

Number of players: Any number, of whom one is banker.

Cards: A 40-card deck is used, with 8s, 9s and 10s stripped out.

The deal: The banker draws two cards from the bottom of the pack, and places them on the table to form the bottom layout. He then deals the top two cards to form the top layout. They will look something like this:

 **Top layout**

 **Bottom layout**

The betting: Bets are placed on the top or bottom layout, up to an agreed maximum. The players are betting that the next card turned up will be of the same suit as one of the cards in the layout betted on. For example, if a player bet on the bottom layout, he would win if the next card was a heart or a diamond.

The play: The banker turns over the pack. The card exposed is the one on which winnings are paid out.

In the diagram, if the next card turned up was a heart, the payout would be on all bets; if it were a spade, the banker would take all the bets.

When played in a casino, the house takes 12½ per cent of all banker's winnings.

The bank itself is passed on every five hands.

110

The Poker Family

Anyone who has seen a Western film will know about Poker. It is the most widely played card game in the world today. It is also the most heavily betted on. In casinos around the globe millions of pounds and dollars change hands over the Poker table.

There was a time when Poker conjured up an image of smoky clubs and illicit drinking, with hard-headed gangsters fingering their guns as well as their cards. This is no longer the case, and there are now more women than men who play the game. Poker has emerged from its disreputable past and become respectable.

Perhaps this is because, contrary to the beginner's vision of it, Poker is a game of skill rather than luck. If you are a good card player, you will stand to win more money playing Poker than any other game.

No one knows exactly where Poker comes from. It may have a European heritage, or it may simply have appeared, the brainchild of some early American pioneer.

There are now countless versions, but with certain basic principles which run through all of them. To play Poker, it is essential to know these principles.

The Principles of Poker

Number of players: Two to eight, playing as individuals.

Cards: One normal pack is used. For some games, two Jokers are added as wild cards.

Objective: To win money (or matchsticks, or whatever betting currency you wish to use). All bets go into a common pot, and the highest hand, or the last hand left in when all others have dropped out, wins the pot.

Poker hands: Each Poker hand contains five cards, which must fall into one of the following categories. Starting with the strongest, they are:

1   ***Royal flush*** – the top five cards in a suit.

Odds on being dealt such a hand: 1 in 649 740.

2   ***Straight flush*** – five cards in sequence in the same suit.

Odds on being dealt such a hand: 1 in 72 193.

3   ***Four of a kind*** – four cards of the same rank, one odd card.

Odds on being dealt such a hand: 1 in 4165.

Don't despair if you hold a pair. In 1975, in the World Series of Poker, Brian Roberts held just that – two Jacks. With them he won $115 500.

4 **Full house** – three cards of the same rank, plus a pair.

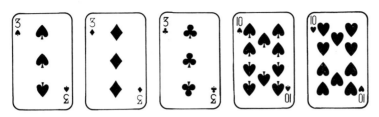

Odds on being dealt such a hand: 1 in 694.

5 **Flush** – five cards of the same suit.

Odds on being dealt such a hand: 1 in 509.

6 **Straight** – five cards in sequence, any suits.

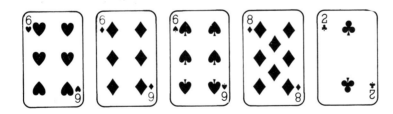

Odds on being dealt such a hand: 1 in 255.

7 **Three of a kind** – three cards of the same rank, two odd cards.

Odds on being dealt such a hand: 1 in 47.

8　**Two pairs** – two pairs and one odd card.

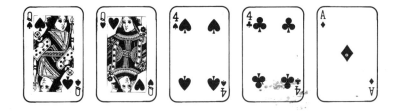

Odds on being dealt such a hand: 1 in 21.

9　**One pair** – one pair and three odd cards.

Odds on being dealt such a hand: 1 in 2.36.

10　**High-card** – no matches or combinations.

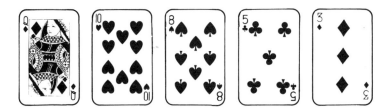

Odds on being dealt such a hand: 1 in 2.

Looked at another way, over 90 per cent of all Poker hands, when first dealt, contain nothing better than a pair.

If there are two hands containing the same combinations, the ranks of the cards are taken into account. For straights, flushes and high-card, the hand with the highest card wins. For hands containing four or three of a kind, the highest ranked group wins; with a full house, it is the rank of the three-group which is decisive.

With two pairs, the higher are compared, then the lower if necessary. If both pairs are identical, the hand containing the higher-ranked odd card wins.

It is similar for hands containing a single pair. If the pairs are identical, the highest odd cards are compared, and so on down to the lowest if there is still no difference.

Suits are irrelevant in the comparisons.

If two hands really are identical, then the pot is split.

Betting: Betting in Poker deserves a special section, which follows at the bottom of the page.

Wild cards: Some games are played with wild cards, which can be used instead of any card of any suit. Normally, jokers or 2s are used. When wild cards are in play, the highest hand becomes five of a kind. Otherwise the hands are ranked in the same order.

The play: This varies from game to game, but will always involve the deal, betting, and the showdown, when the hands are exposed and the pot is claimed.

Types of poker: There are two main forms, Draw poker and Stud poker, each of which has spawned numerous variations, some of which are looked at in the section *Dealer's Choice* (page 120); for in many card schools the player who cuts the cards and becomes dealer has the choice of playing any form of Poker he wishes, regardless of how obscure it is.

Betting in Poker

Betting is the very heart of Poker. Without betting, Poker would die. There are certain guidelines which have become established over a number of years – they may vary slightly from game to game, but in general they follow these principles:

Rounds of betting: There will always be at least one, and often several, rounds of betting. The first round starts after the players have received their cards.

Betting options: Every player has the opportunity to bet, with the following options:

1 *Fold* – a player throws in his cards and takes no further part in the hand. A player can fold on any round of the betting.

2 *Stay in* – a player matches the highest bet so far, and waits for further developments.

3 *Raise* – a player bets enough chips to stay in, then puts in some more, forcing other players to match the new total, or fold.

4 *Check* – if a new round of betting has started but no one has raised, a player can stay in without placing a further bet. However, should anyone else choose to raise, the checker must then match the amount or fold.

Ending a round of betting: This happens when all players have checked, all bar one player have dropped out (in which case he takes the pot), or all players have equalized their bets.

　　If everyone checks on the first round of betting, the deal is void and the cards are passed on to the next dealer.

Poker can be compulsive. In 1853 two planters from Austin, Texas began playing. They continued throughout the Civil War and the Reconstruction, ending only when they both died simultaneously twenty years later.

Other betting rules: There are numerous additional rules for betting which you may or may not wish to adopt, depending on the seriousness of your game and the size of your salary (or pocket money!).

1   *Side bets* between players can be introduced. For example, on the location of a particular card.
2   *Bonuses* can be agreed before play, with extra amounts being paid out by all players for certain hands, such as straight flushes.
3   *A betting limit* is normal. This can be in the form of a limit on the amount of a raise, a limit on the value of the pot, or simply by allowing a limited amount of money to circulate in the game.
4   *Betting chips* are easier to handle during the game than money. Different coloured chips are needed to represent different amounts of money.
5   *Borrowing* money or chips during a game is not allowed, nor can players bet for another player.
6   *Sandbagging* (continually raising until other players run out of money) is an unscrupulous player's trick.

To prevent it, a player can bet a *freezing raise* – this is twice the normal maximum raise, and ends the betting.

Draw Poker

The distinguishing feature of Draw poker is the exchange of cards which takes place after the first round of betting. It is the form of poker which everyone knows how to play, although the big-money players prefer Stud poker.

Number of players: Two to ten can play, although the best number is four to six.

Cards: One normal pack is used, with no wild cards.

Initial stake: Each player must place a small compulsory bet, agreed before the deal.

The deal: Five cards are dealt to each player.

First round of betting: Each player, having looked at his hand, must bet or fold. Checking is not allowed. The player to the dealer's left is first to speak.

If everyone folds, the compulsory bets for the next hand are added to the existing pot, and the cards are passed to the next dealer.

It may be that the pot is won in the first round of betting, if only one player is prepared to bet, or if everyone has dropped out after a series of raises. Otherwise the draw takes place.

The draw: Starting with the first player to the dealer's left who has not folded, each has the chance to exchange up to three cards from his hand. If a player wishes to draw, he states the number of cards required, and discards those not needed. The dealer then gives the player the correct number of cards, dealt from the top of the pack.

If a player does not wish to draw, he knocks the table.

These rules apply in exactly the same way for the dealer.

If the bottom card of the pack is reached, it is shuffled together with the discarded cards to form new stock.

Second round of betting: The same rules apply as for the first round, except that this time checking is allowed.

If all bar one player drop out, he wins the pot. Otherwise a situation arises where everyone has checked, or two or more players have equalized bets. In both cases, the showdown takes place.

The showdown: Each player who is still active must place his hand face up on the table, announcing its value as he does so. The player with the highest hand takes the pot.

Strategy: There are two main areas of skill. The first is purely mathematical, the second concerns the player's personality!

Since the only cards that you can see are your own, it is possible to work out exactly what the chances are of picking up a particular card or cards at any time.

Here are a few samples:

1 *Chance of improving a pair* by picking three cards (for example, three of a kind, or two pairs): 1 in 3½.
2 *Chance of improving three of a kind* by picking two cards (four of a kind or a full house): 1 in 10.
3 *Chance of filling a straight* such as Q, J, 10, 8 by picking one card (must be a 9): 1 in 12.

It is an interesting exercise to work out the odds for each type of combination.

Bluffing is a vital part of Poker. If you can convince your adversaries that you have a good hand, they may drop out without ever putting your hand to the test. This can be done in two ways, either through your general manner, or through the way you approach the draw. If you have only a pair, but change two cards rather than three, everyone will take you for something better. But remember, never let on that you are bluffing, and always keep a poker face!

Sample Game – Draw Poker

Fresh from their game of Blackjack, our heroes turn their hands to poker – Timid Tim, Reckless Ruth, Stupid Sam, Positive Pete and Mathematical Moira.

Each of them puts one chip into the pot, then Moira deals.
The hands are as follows:

Tim	4C, 4H, 9S, 3S, QH
Ruth	QS, QC, 2C, 2D, AH
Sam	JC, JD, 10H, 8D, 5D
Pete	AS, AD, 6S, 6D, 3H
Moira	KH, KD, 3D, 7D, 2S

First round of betting

Tim immediately folds, as he does on virtually every hand; in his opinion a pair of fours is far too weak. The problem is, on the infrequent occasions that Tim stays in, everyone knows he is holding something spectacular so they drop out, and he wins a feeble little pot with a big powerful hand.

Ruth has no such misgivings. She has a good hand, and decides to start by putting two chips into the pot.

Sam will bet on anything, and as he sees it, this is a very promising hand –

117

he has the choice of going for more Jacks, or discarding JC and 10H in the hope of completing a flush. He puts in two chips, and raises two.

Pete likes his hand. He has high hopes of winning a substantial pot, but obviously he doesn't want to scare anyone off at this stage. He puts in four, which is now the level of the pot, and raises two.

Moira thinks awhile. Two Kings is not great, but a third one would make for a strong hand. She decides to stay in for the moment, but with some misgivings. She puts in six.

Ruth puts in four, then raises six (total twelve).

Sam matches her bet by putting in eight.

Pete also equalizes bets, by putting in six.

Moira folds, concluding the first round of betting.

There are now forty-seven chips in the pot – five from the compulsory bets, and a further forty-two put in during the first round of betting.

The draw:

Ruth asks for one card, discards AH and is dealt AC. Her final hand is: QS, QC, 2D, 2C, AC.

Sam decides to go for the Jacks. He asks for three cards, hands over 10H, 8D, 5D and is dealt KS, 9C, 7C – unlucky!

Pete asks for one, hands over 3H and is dealt 6C. He now has a full house: 6S, 6D, 6C, AS, AD.

Second round of betting

Ruth has got the bit between her teeth. She may not have got the card she wanted, but that isn't going to stop her now. She puts in five chips to start the betting.

Sam may be stupid, but he is not a total idiot, nor is he an inveterate bluffer. He folds.

Pete is a very confident now. But he must not frighten Ruth off. He is like an angler, gradually hauling in the money. He puts in five, and raises five.

Ruth puts in five, and raises ten – maybe she can scare Pete!

Pete puts in ten and raises five.

Ruth puts in five and raises ten. If at first you don't succeed . . .

Pete puts in ten and raises five.

Ruth has had enough. She equalizes bets and they compare hands.

The total pot is worth 127 chips, with Ruth losing 54 of them.

It is 2 August 1876. A Poker game is in progress in a Deadwood saloon. One of the players is famed Western hero Wild Bill Hickok. Suddenly the door bursts open, and a young gunslinger named Jack McCall strides in.

A moment later a shot rings out, and Wild Bill slumps over the table, a bullet lodged in the back of his head. His cards fall with him, two pairs, Aces and 8s.

Ever since that day, such a combination has been known as 'the Dead Man's Hand'.

Stud Poker

There is more scope for working out mathematical probabilities in Stud poker than in Draw poker, thus it is a game of greater skill. There is no exchange of cards.

Number of players: Two to ten.

Cards: One normal pack is used, with no wild cards.

Initial stake: Each player must place a small compulsory bet before the cards are dealt.

The deal: One card is dealt face down to each player (the *hole card*), then a second is dealt face up, overlapping the first. The hole card cannot be looked at before the showdown.

First round of betting: The player with the highest exposed card, or in the case of duplicates, the player nearer the dealer's left, opens the betting. Each player can bet or fold, with the betting round ending when all bets are equalized, after the usual raising, re-raising and so on.

Continuation: A further card is dealt, face up, to each player still in the game. Then another round of betting takes place. This continues until each remaining player has four cards face up, plus the hole card.

For each round, the order of betting is determined by the relative ranking of the incomplete hands.

Once each player has five cards, and the betting has concluded, the showdown takes place, with players exposing their hole cards and comparing their hands.

Players can fold on any round of betting. If they do so, they turn all their cards face down. The hole card should *not* be exposed. If all players bar one drop out, he wins the pot.

Strategy: The bluff element is smaller than in Draw poker, but the skill element is larger, with the odds on helpful cards appearing being calculable at each round.

Several American presidents have been keen Poker players. Harry Truman liked unorthodox variations, whilst Franklin D. Roosevelt once went direct from a Poker game to give one of his famous fireside chats. The whole nation listened, perplexed, while the President absent-mindedly clicked his Poker chips so noisily that his words were obliterated.

Dealer's Choice

So, you are the dealer, and you want to find a version of Poker which is different, fun to play and might just knock your fellow players out of their stride. The following selection should give you a few ideas. But one last piece of advice: only choose the penultimate game if you are playing Poker with *very* good friends!

Jacks or Better

Identical to straight Draw poker, but with the restriction that a player can only open betting with a hand containing two Jacks or better. Thereafter other players can bet as normal. At the end of the first round of betting, before the draw, the player who has opened must show his hand to the other players.

Poker with a Five-Card Draw

Unlike the standard game, up to five cards can be drawn, rather than three. Poker can also be played with a **four-card draw** maximum.

Draw Poker with Wild Cards

In **Twos wild**, the four 2s are wild cards and can be used in lieu of any card. In **Jokers wild**, two Jokers are added to the pack and become wild. Alternatively, why not have all six as wild cards?

Fives and tens is a little more complicated. All the 5s and 10s are wild cards, but in order to start the betting a player must have at least one 5 and one 10 in his hand. This means that a lot of hands are thrown in! It also means that the average winning hand is at least four of a kind, and five of a kind or a straight flush are not uncommon.

Lowball

The rules of play in Lowball are identical to Draw poker, but the lowest hand wins. Aces count low. Straights and flushes do not score in Lowball, so the lowest possible hand is A, 2, 3, 4, 5. One Joker, *the bug*, is usually added to the pack and can be used as any card.

High-Low Draw Poker

This is straight Draw poker, but with the pot divided evenly between the highest and lowest hands. An interesting variation is **Seven-card high-low draw poker**. Each player is dealt seven cards, betting takes place, then each passes three cards to the player on his left. The players then select the best (or worst) hand they can from the seven cards they now hold, then the showdown takes place, with the pot split between the high and low hands.

Rockleigh

Another variation on the High-low theme. Each player is dealt four cards, then four extra two-card groups are dealt face down in the centre of the table. The players look at their hands, then a betting round takes place. The dealer then turns over the first two-card group, and a further round of betting takes place. The procedure is repeated for each group. Once all four have been turned up, the showdown takes place, with each player able to perm five out of six with any group, to select their highest and lowest hands. Thus it is quite possible for a player to win high and low, using two different groups.

One-Card Poker

This is Poker for the simpleton, or perhaps just the habitually lazy. One card is dealt to each player. Betting then takes place for high or low. **Two-card poker** is a more advanced version, where the best possible hand is a pair of Aces.

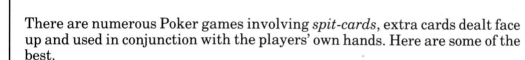

There are numerous Poker games involving *spit-cards*, extra cards dealt face up and used in conjunction with the players' own hands. Here are some of the best.

Spit in the Ocean

Each player is dealt four cards, then a single card is dealt face up in the centre of the table. This always comprises the fifth card for every player's hand. A round of betting takes place based on the first four cards, then cards are exchanged as in Draw poker. A second round of betting follows, then the showdown.

Pig in the Poke

This is a variation on Spit in the ocean. The players are dealt four cards, with one in the centre face up. However, the three cards of the same rank as the spit-card are wild. For example, if the card in the centre is 6D, then it retains that value, but if you hold 6H, you can substitute it for any card you wish.

Some players prefer to have the centre card itself wild, as well as its three companions of like rank.

In **Wild widow**, the players are dealt five cards, but an extra one is turned up and sets the rank of the wild cards, as in Pig in the poke.

Both these games have two rounds of betting and a draw, as in the standard game.

Stormy Weather

Players are dealt four cards, and three extra cards are dealt face down on the table. A round of betting takes place after the players have looked at their initial cards. The three additional cards are then turned up, one at a time, with a round of betting taking place as each is turned. In the showdown, the players can use any of the three to combine with their own hand. There is a draw after the first round of betting.

Lame Brain

This game is also known as **Confusion**, which is probably a more appropriate name. Five cards are dealt to each player, and five extra cards are dealt face down in the centre of the table. There is no draw. The first of the five cards is turned up, and players start to place bets. Once the betting round is complete, the second card is turned up, and the process repeated. Eventually all five cards are face up, and five rounds of betting have taken place. In the showdown, each player can make up the best possible hand from their own five cards, plus the five on the table.

In **Round the world**, only four cards are dealt to hand, and four to the table. Otherwise the game is identical to Lame brain.

High-low and Wild card variations can be adapted equally well to Stud poker, but the most popular variant is the seven-card version.

Seven-Card Stud Poker

Two cards are dealt face down to each player, then one face up. The four rounds of betting taking place as in standard Stud poker, then a seventh card is dealt face down. In the showdown, the players are able to construct the best possible hand from the seven cards.

Six-car stud is the same except that only the first and last cards dealt are face down, with the four in between face up.

In **English seven-card stud**, after five rounds, when each player has two cards face down and three face up, one replacement card can be drawn, followed by an extra round of betting. Otherwise the game is the same.

Crazy Five-Card High-Low Stud

This is played in the same way as standard Stud, but with the following additional rules:
1 After the hole cards have been dealt, the dealer gives the player to his left one card face up. This player can keep the card, or pass it on to the player on

his left. If he passes it on, he is dealt a second card face up which he must keep. If he keeps it, the second player is dealt one card, and he likewise can keep it or pass it on. This process continues around the table, until everyone has two cards. The dealer himself can discard a card passed to him; if so, he deals himself the top card from the pack in its place.

The next three rounds are normal, then comes the showdown. . . .

2   When each player has five cards, they can discard any one card, either the hole card or any of the face-up ones, and be dealt another in its place. Another round of betting can then take place.

The pot is divided evenly between the high and low hands.

Pass the Rubbish

Seven cards are dealt, face down, to each player. A round of betting takes place, then each player passes three cards to the player on his left. There is another round of betting, then each player discards two cards. Before the showdown, the top four cards of the pack are turned up one at a time, with a further round of betting after each turn-up. Finally, the hands are compared, using the best five from the nine cards on show, five in hand and four on the table.

Strip Poker

No money is required, just a bit of cheek and plenty of clothing. Draw poker is played, with everyone participating in every hand. In the showdown, the player with the lowest hand must remove one article of clothing. How the game ends depends on the players!

The most famous Poker club in history was the Round Table Group who met at the Algonquin Hotel in New York. Among its members were Jerome Kern, Robert Benchley, Paul Robeson and Harpo Marx. Harpo was once reputed to have won $30 000 in one game.

Three-Card Brag

Brag is an old English ancestor of Poker. It developed from the much earlier card game Primero (see page 21). There are several versions, but by far the most popular is Three-card brag.

Number of players: Three to twelve.

Cards: One normal pack is used, no wild cards. Ace is high.

Initial stake: Each player puts one chip into the pot.

The deal: Three cards are dealt to each player.

Brag hands: There is no exchange of cards in Brag; you must play with the three cards dealt. The ranking of hands, starting with the highest, is as follows:

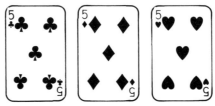

1 **Pryle** – three cards of the same rank. The highest pryle is three 3s. Then come three Aces, three Kings and so on.

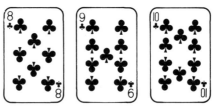

2 **On a bike run** – three cards in sequence in the same suit.

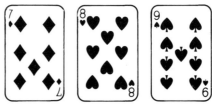

3 **Run** – three cards in sequence, regardless of suit.

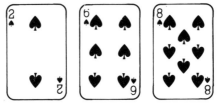

4 **Flush** – three cards of the same suit.

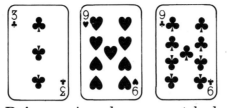

5   ***Pair*** – a pair and one unmatched card.

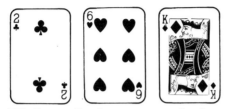

6   ***High card*** – three unmatched cards.

Hands of the same rank are valued as in Poker (page 112).

The betting: Starting with the player to the dealer's left, each player has the chance to bet or drop out, known as *stacking*. A player can look at his hand, in which case he is said to be *open*. Or he can bet blind, without knowing its contents. If any player is betting blind, an open player must pay double the blind man's bet. A showdown cannot take place until there are only two players left in. At this point, if one wishes to invoke the showdown, he must double the last bet and say 'I'll see you.' However, an open better cannot see a blind man – he can only continue to match bets.

   The winning hand takes the pot.

Cheating at Cards

There are many different types of card cheat.

The least harmful is the person who cheats only himself; the type who bends the rules at a game of Patience, in order to get out. No one suffers, but such a person displays a sad lack of moral fibre.

Then there is the amateur cheat, the person who deliberately adds up the score incorrectly, or surreptitiously removes part of his bet when he realizes that the cards are not favouring him. Such people are irritating and worth trying to avoid in a card game, but they are not too much of a problem. Their ploys are generally clumsy, and can be detected and corrected. Embarrassment may be caused, but must be endured if your finances are to remain intact.

The real danger is the professional cheat. Professional card cheats come in two forms:

1 Those who manipulate the pack.
2 Those who signal to other players, either in a partnership game, or in a gambling game where two or more players can act in tandem with each other.

Card Manipulation

A person who manipulates the cards is known as a card sharp. He is not a miracle maker. Unless the cards have been previously stacked, he cannot automatically deal four-of-a-kind to each player in a game of Poker. The art of the card sharp is to know where in the pack one or two cards are. This is sufficient to give him an edge, and if he has an edge he will win your money.

There is one very important giveaway of the card sharp – the way in which he holds the pack. If you see a player holding the deck with three fingers on the long side, the index finger at the end, and the thumb over the top, then it is time to leave the game.

This method of holding the pack, which is known as 'the mechanic's grip' is essential for many of the main manouevres of the card sharp. Here are some that you should look out for:

Peeping at the top card: pressure is exerted by the thumb, so that the card bends slightly. This causes the corner to come up just enough for the card sharp to take a look.

The bottom deal: the dealer pushes the top card slightly over with his thumb, while at the same time slipping the card off the bottom of the pack with his other hand, which appears to be taking the top card.

The second deal: this is similar to the bottom deal, but is slightly easier to execute. The top card is pushed out, but the second card is actually extracted.

127

Before each of these manouevres, the card sharp will have stacked the deck so that certain cards are in certain positions. This is how it is done:

The pickup stack: generally when a hand ends there will be certain cards lying face up on the table. The card sharp ensures that the ones he wants are in the right places in the pack, say fourth and eighth, through picking them up in a particular order, and placing them at the top of the deck. You might think that the shuffle and cut of the pack will kill his plans, but the clever card sharp has all the answers. . . .

False shuffles: there are several methods, all of which give the impression of shuffling, but do not change the positions of any critical cards.

One of the most popular shuffles is the Pull Through. In order to execute it the card sharp divides the pack into two sections, riffles them together, then whips the two sections of the pack through each other in such a way that he appears to be making a legitimate cut. In fact the position of every card remains identical.

Nullifying the cut: the simplest method is to avoid cutting altogether, and it is surprising how often a card cheat can get away with this. Alternatively, he will allow a player to cut the pack, and will then replace the two cut portions so that the pack is restored to the state it was before the cut.

Another favourite method is *crimping* a card. This means bending it slightly, so that the cutter is inadvertently attracted to that card; his fingers conveniently find the crimped card. Before the cut, the cheat crimps the card which he wants at the top, then places approximately half the deck on top of it. The trap is set.

A third method is for the sharp to employ an accomplice, a second player who positions himself next to the cheat, and pretends to cut but does not actually do so. This distracts attention from the card sharp himself.

There are other less subtle ways in which the card sharp may be at work, such as using pre-arranged decks, palming cards or using marked cards.

The prearranged deck: This is a tool which the professional card cheat will use only once, but which can bring him immense dividends. During the game he will leave for a few moments, during which he prepares a deck, identical to one being used in the game, so that the cards are stacked in an order designed to lure his victims into large, losing bets. At a convenient moment, the prearranged deck will be introduced into the game.

There is one big giveaway. The cards will invariably be colder than the pack which has been in use, hence the description of a prearranged pack as a *cold deck*.

Palming cards: This is the best known and most easily detected form of cheating. It is risky, but the card sharp will use it if the other players seem particularly naïve or inexperienced.

At the end of a deal, while cards are lying face up on the table, the cheat will remove the card he wants by secreting it in the hollow formed by the palm of his hand. At the same time, he will distract attention by reaching for a handkerchief or cigarette with his other hand. The card is then concealed in his armpit, or under his knee, until it is required, at which point the cheat substitutes it for one of the cards in his hand.

Marked cards: Marked cards are cards whose values can be ascertained by looking at their backs. It is estimated that one out of every hundred packs sold are, at some stage, doctored so as to be readable from the back. This can happen before the cards are sold, with packs being broken open, marked, then resealed. In one well-documented incident, during the races at Saratoga in America, a whole shipment of cards was tampered with, and hundreds of people ended up being duped with their own cards which they had just bought.

There are many things to look for if you believe that a pack of cards is marked. Here are some:

1   *Edge work* – where cards have a white margin, the line between the margin and the back design is thickened up slightly, high up for an Ace, a little lower for a King, and so on.

An example of edge work.

2   **Line work** – extra lines are added to the back design. The more complicated the design, the easier it is to do.
3   **Cut-out or Blocking** – small areas of black are scratched out, or painted white. Alternatively, extra spots of black are added.
4   **Shading** – white areas are shaded grey, high up for an Ace, lower for a King and so on. To the layman, it looks merely as though the cards are a little dirty.
5   **Trims** – again where cards have a white margin; the high cards are trimmed so that one margin is wider than the other. The low and unimportant cards are then trimmed half the amount at both sides, so that all cards are the same size.

Of course these markings are very subtle, and require a trained eye to spot them.

Even if you are playing with a pack which you know to be unmarked, the card marker might soon change things. There are various ways in which he can change the markings on cards during the course of the game.

He can dig his nail into the side of the card, high up for an Ace, and a little further down for lower cards. He can daub the card with a yellow wax, so that the mark is similar to a nicotine stain. It is even possible for the cheat to hide a tiny tack in a finger bandage, which he can then use to prick the cards.

The sign of a card marker is a tendency to concentrate on the backs of the cards, rather than the fronts. Watch out for it!

If you want to see marked cards being used to fleece innocent people, then search out a game of Three-card monte, but be warned; don't be tempted to take part!

Three-card monte is a game, or more accurately a swindle, in which a card sharp shows his victims three cards, two red Aces and the Queen of Spades, then throws them down and invites anyone to place a bet which wins if the Queen of Spades is successfully located. The cards are invariably fixed, with the Queen of Spades unsubtly marked. This is card-marking in reverse, because the unsuspecting victim is supposed to spot the mark. He then places his bet, confident that he can pick out the Queen of Spades regardless of the card sharp's manipulation of the cards.

There is just one problem. Between showing the cards and throwing them down, the card sharp substitutes an unmarked Queen of Spades, and an Ace marked exactly like the card which the better has spotted.

The result is money thrown away. A famed Canberra gambler once said of Three-card monte, 'It would not seem possible to find anyone so densely ignorant as to make a wager on it.'

129

Signalling

In a big money Poker game, it is not unusual to find a player with an accomplice who will find a seat where he can see at least two of the other players' hands. The accomplice then signals to his partner, giving signs which are translated and used to determine betting strategy.

For this reason, it is wise to position yourself where no one can look over your shoulder.

Having said this, there is actually a very narrow line between bluffing and cheating at poker. A good bluffer might announce, when it is not his turn, that he plans to drop out. Then when the play comes round to him, he raises. Alternatively, he might make out that his hand is powerful, in the hope that everyone drops out and leaves him the pot, whereas his real intention is to throw in his hand as soon as the opportunity arises. These are valid bluffs. Hiring an assistant to sit behind him and give false indications of his hand would be cheating.

Cheating at Bridge

At Bridge, or any partnership game, the card cheat is given an additional opportunity to do his wicked deeds. The cards themselves can still be fixed, but there is also the opportunity for a cheat to convey information illegally to his partner. Of course this requires two cheats rather than one.

The illegal transfer of information can occur in several ways:

1 **Kicking under the table** – old-fashioned and unsubtle, this would hardly go on at anything other than informal Bridge sessions. The risk of kicking the wrong person is far too high!

2 **Voice intonations** – during the bidding, the tone in which something is said can convey information. Again, this is unsubtle and easily spotted. The problem is distinguishing between mannerisms and cheating.

3 **Non-verbal mannerisms** – a scratch of the ear, a tug of the hair, a sucking of the lips; none seem suspicious, yet all could pass on information.

4 **Finger signals** – players can hold their cards with different numbers of fingers showing. The number showing could be used to represent the number of cards in a particular suit.

In the late 1960s there was a famous incident in the World Bridge Championships, when a British partnership was accused by their American opponents of doing exactly that. Nothing was proved, but the Bridge world took a long time to recover from the accusation. Even now, there is ill-feeling between some of the players involved.

The Gordon-Cumming Affair

The most famous cheating incident in the history of card playing was a Royal scandal in Britain.

In Victorian times, betting on cards was illegal. Despite this, the Prince of Wales, later to become Edward VII, introduced Baccarat to the court, where it rapidly found favour amongst the aristocracy.

At one of their weekend sessions, a Scottish baronet and landowner, Sir William Gordon-Cumming, joined the game. He began to prosper, and afterwards suspicions were expressed about the honesty of his play. The following day he was observed more closely, and was apparently caught changing his bet after the stakes had been finalized. He was asked to leave the game, and everyone agreed not to mention the incident, providing Gordon-Cumming promised not to take part in any more card games.

The affair seemed to be resolved, but gradually word reached Gordon-Cumming that rumours of his disgrace were circulating the court, and he decided that he would attempt to restore his reputation, for he had always maintained his innocence.

He demanded retractions of the allegations, and a court case followed, with the Prince of Wales called to give evidence. The case ended with Gordon-Cumming found guilty. He was ostracized from society, but the most serious repercussion was that Queen Victoria's son had been shown to be a gambler, a fact which pained the monarch and brought considerable embarrassment to the Royal household.

131

Many a cheat has met with a violent death. In the Wild West, it was common practice to deal with the left hand so as to leave the right free to whip out a gun should an adversary be caught cheating.

Things are rather more genteel these days, but a cheat is still despised. If you are guilty of illegal practices yourself, and cannot turn to a straight and honest road, then at least you might consider turning to a game where the main objective is to cheat.

Cheat

Any number of players can play, and all cards are dealt out. The objective is to get rid of all your cards by placing them face down on a sequential discard heap, announcing their values as you do so. Of course the rank announced need not be the same as the rank of the card placed! But if you are accused and found guilty of cheating, you are forced to pick up the discard heap and add it to your hand. An incorrect accusation results in the accuser picking up the discard heap.

The first player to get rid of all his cards is the winner, and becomes the Champion Cheat!

The Rummy Family

Along with Bridge and Poker, Rummy is one of the big three in the family of card games.

Its heritage is uncertain. It may have been born in Mexico, as a descendant of the ancient game Con Quian, but it is more likely that it developed from Poker. If so, then its birthplace was the saloon bars and gambling halls of late-nineteenth-century America. It was a time when cards were frowned on, and card players were hard living, heavy drinking, disreputable types.

The name Rummy comes directly from rum – as well as drinking it, the pioneer card players would also use it as their betting currency.

There are numerous members of the Rummy family, many of which might claim to be the original game. However, the majority of people who talk simply of playing Rummy are referring to the straight seven-card version, and since it illustrates the principles of the game admirably, I shall use it as my basic model.

♥ ♣ ♦ ♠

Seven-Card Rummy

Number of players: Two to eight.

Cards: One normal pack is used for two to eight players. Two packs are used if there are more than four players. Aces are low.

Objective: To get rid of all the cards in your hand, by forming matching sets known as *melds*. These can be three or more cards of the same rank (for example 6S, 6H, and 6C) or three or more cards of the same suit, in sequence (for example 8D, 9D, 10D, JD).

The deal: Each player is dealt seven cards. The remainder of the pack forms a face-down stock pile, the top card of which is turned up and placed alongside, to form the base of a discard pile.

The play: The player to the dealer's left starts; thereafter play rotates in a clockwise direction.

A player's turn comprises three elements: *draw*, *meld* and *discard*.

First, the player draws a card, either from the top of the stock pile, or from the top of the discard pile.

He adds the card to his hand and, if he is able to and wishes to, he can lay down on the table any melds which he is able to form. He is also able to add cards to melds formed by other players, known as *laying off*. For example, if he holds 6D, and elsewhere on the table there is a three-card run of 7D, 8D, 9D, he can place 6D to the left of this sequence, extending it to four cards. There are no limits on the length of the sequence, or the number of cards which can be laid off to a meld. Any cards placed on the table should be spread out so that all are visible. It is perfectly legitimate for players to hold melds within their hands, rather than spreading them on the table.

Finally, the player concludes his turn by discarding a card face up on the top of the discard pile.

The hand ends as soon as one player uses up all his cards, with or without the final discard.

If the stock is exhausted before any player has gone out, the discard pile is turned over and used as the new stock pile.

If a player goes out in one move, without previously placing any melds or laying off any cards, he is said to have *gone rummy*.

The scoring: The player who has gone out receives the numerical value of all the cards in his opponent's hands, with court cards counting as ten points each. If a player has gone rummy, the points are doubled.

A game is played up to any previously agreed total, perhaps 100 or 500 points, depending on the time at your disposal.

Strategy: Rummy is largely a game of observation. It may not be possible to control the order of the cards, but it is possible to watch them as they appear, and alter one's strategy accordingly. For example, if you have been waiting for a particular card, then see it discarded and buried, obviously there is no point in hanging on to the combination requiring that card.

It is also worthwhile observing the other players. Someone who picks a card from stock, and immediately discards it, looks very much as though he needs only one card for success. If that is the case, it is best to lay out any melds in your hand, so as not to get caught with them when the scoring takes place.

Similarly, avoid holding too many high-scoring cards. If you have a meld of court cards, such as three Queens, it may be sensible to play them, especially if someone is showing signs of going out. Likewise, discard a high-scoring card rather than a low-scoring one, if neither is required.

Finally, avoid giving away your own position. Always draw, add the card to your hand, then discard at an even tempo, whether you are almost out, or nowhere near.

Sample Game – Seven-Card Rummy

There are four players, Arthur, Brenda, Cathy and Dave, also known as A, B, C and D.

Arthur deals, and the cards come out as follows:

	A	B	C	D
Spades	10, 4	9	A	J
Hearts	7, 6	K, 9, 8	–	Q, 4
Diamonds	J, 4	Q	6, 5, 2, A	K, 7
Clubs	9	3, A	Q, J	10, 8

This in itself is somewhat misleading. In Rummy, cards are not sorted primarily in suits, they are sorted into potential melds; cards of the same rank, or part sequences.

The card turned up is 9D.

Round 1

Brenda takes 9D, creating a set of three 9s. She discards KH, a high-scoring card which she does not require.

Cathy has no need of KH. She picks 6C from stock. There is no obvious discard, but eventually she decides on 2D. Why? Because the only card which will create a meld, should 2D be kept, is 3D. For each of the other combinations, there are two possible cards which will create a meld.

Dave decides to pick from stock, and gets 5H, a potentially useful card. He discards KD.

Arthur also picks from stock, receiving 5S. He discards JD.

Round 2

Brenda's hand is looking quite promising. She picks JD to go with QD, and discards 8H, since 9H is now tied up in a set. As yet, she has no desire to place her set on the table.

Cathy picks from stock, and strikes lucky: KC, completing the sequence JC, QC, KC. She must now find a discard from AS, 6D, 5D, AD and 6C. Again, it is a difficult choice. She decides on 5D, keeping the two pairs.

Dave takes 5D and discards QH. He is still a long way from anything useful.

Arthur picks from stock, getting 2S – not particularly helpful, but he keeps it and discards 10S.

The hands are now as follows:

Arthur **S** 5, 4, 2 **H** 7, 6 **D** 4 **C** 9
Brenda **S** 9 **H** 9 **D** Q, J, 9 **C** 3, A
Cathy   **S** A **H** – **D** 6, A **C** K, Q, J, 6
Dave   **S** J **H** 5, 4 **D** 7, 5 **C** 10, 8

Round 3
Brenda picks 6S from stock, then, after a suitable interval, discards it.

Cathy is almost out. She takes 6S, completing a set of three. She still has no thoughts of playing any cards on to the table; her thoughts are on going rummy. She discards AD.

Dave picks 4C from stock, and discards JS.

Arthur picks 3H from stock. It is no use to him, but he discards the higher-scoring 9C.

Round 4
Brenda's fourth 9! She takes it, and discards QD – she has remembered that KD was discarded earlier.

Cathy picks 3D from stock, and discards AS.

Dave picks AH from stock, and discards 10C; he had been waiting for 9C, but has just seen it picked up by Brenda.

Arthur picks 10D from stock, then promptly discards it.

The four hands are now as follows:

Arthur **S** 5, 4, 2 **H** 7, 6, 3 **D** 4 **C** –
Brenda **S** 9 **H** 9 **D** J, 9 **C** 9, 3, A
Cathy   **S** 6 **H** – **D** 6, 3 **C** K, Q, J, 6
Dave   **S** – **H** 5, 4, A **D** 7, 5 **C** 8, 4

Round 5
Brenda picks 10H from stock, discarding JD.

Cathy picks 8D from stock, then lays down JC, QC, KC. She has seen 10C discarded, so there is no point in waiting for that card. Also, the longer the game goes on, the more chance there is of someone else going rummy, and she doesn't want to get caught with a handful of high-scoring cards! She decides to hold on to her 6s, and discards 8D.

Dave takes 8D, which combines with 7D and 8C, then discards AH.

Arthur picks 7S from stock, and discards 3H.

Round 6
Brenda takes 3H and discards 10H. She now has two chances of a card enabling her to go rummy – either 2C or any 3. Her full hand is: **S** 9   **H** 9, 3 **D** 9 **C** 9, 3, A.

Cathy picks 8S from stock, then decides to lay down her 6s, in the hope that others will follow her example and provide her with a place to lay off her final card. She discards 8S, keeping only 3D.

Dave takes 8S, lays down 8S, 8D and 8C, then discards 7D. His hand now reads: **H** 5, 4 **D** 5 **C** 4.

Arthur takes 7D, lays down 7D, 7S and 7H, then discards 6H. He now holds: **S** 5, 4, 2 **D** 4.

Round 7

Brenda picks QS from stock, then lays down her four 9s. She discards QS, leaving herself with H 3 and C 3, A.

Cathy picks and discards KS.

Dave picks 2H – only one card (3H) away from a four-card sequence allowing him to go out. He decides to gamble on it, and throws 5D, leaving himself with H 5, 4, 2 and C 4.

Arthur picks 3S from stock, and is able to lay down S 2, 3, 4, 5, discard 4D and go out. From a fairly hopeless position two turns earlier, he has come back to win the game.

He scores twenty-five points (seven from Brenda, three from Cathy and fifteen from Dave).

There are numerous variations on straight Seven-card rummy. **Six-card rummy** is identical, except that only six cards are dealt.

In **Block rummy**, the player going out must make a final discard. This can prevent a player winning even when he can meld all his cards, particularly if a six-card version of Block rummy is played.

In **Queen city rummy** a player can only meld if he can play all his cards, although a final discard is not necessary.

Skip rummy is an intriguing variation which involves restricted melding and a five-card deal. The play is identical to standard Rummy, but a player has only two melding options on his turn:

1 *A three-card meld*, either three cards of the same rank, or a three-card sequence of one suit.
2 *One card laid off* on to any meld laid out on the table.

Thus if a player has a four-card meld, he must place it over two turns, three one move, one the next. It is not possible to play a three-card meld *and* a single-card layoff in one turn. When a player has gone rummy, he is paid two chips by each of his opponents: if no one has succeeded in going rummy by the time the stock runs out, the player with the lowest card-count (court cards counting ten) is paid one chip by the other players.

In **Round-the-corner** or **Boathouse rummy**, the Ace can be high or low – or both, so that a sequence of KC, AC, 2C becomes valid. There is an unusual rule for drawing: the top two cards can be drawn from the discard pile, or the top card from both the discard pile and the stock pile, or a single card drawn from the top of stock. Whatever the draw, only one card is discarded.

The discard pile can be shuffled and re-used as stock if no player has gone out before stock is exhausted.

Five Hundred Rummy

The target here is 500 points, scored over any number of hands. The game is also known as **Pinochle rummy**.

Number of players: Two to four.

Cards: One normal pack is used. Ace can be high or low. Each card has its own value, the Ace being worth fifteen points, the court cards ten points each, and the other cards their face values.

The deal: Each player is dealt seven cards. The remainder form a stock pile, the top card of which is turned up to form the base of a discard pile.

The play: The normal procedure of draw, meld and discard applies, but with an important difference. Not only is the top card of the discard pile available; any number can be taken, from the top down, subject to the restriction that the bottom card taken must be used immediately in a meld of at least three cards.

Cards can be laid off to other players' melds, although the card itself is laid down in front of the player playing it, not on the meld itself. For example, if Player one has a meld of 4D, 5D, 6D, Player two could place 7D in front of him and state that it is an extension of Player one's meld. Sometimes there could be ambiguity, so it is important that a player specifies clearly which meld he is adding to. It is also advisable to keep a close eye on the single cards in front of the other players, so as to know what is the current state of each meld.

The hand ends when any one player uses up all his cards.

Scoring: All cards on the table in front of a player constitute plus points; any held in hand are minus points. The difference between the two represents the score on the hand.

Strategy: It is more important to meld cards than to go out, the more cards the better. Try to take the discard pile at every opportunity, if necessary by 'planting' cards which you know you can combine to form melds when it is your turn.

Gin Rummy

Gin rummy is the most popular two-player card game in the world. It was invented at the turn of the century, but reached its peak in the 1930s and 1940s when it was widely played in Hollywood and became known as 'The Game of the Stars'.

In America Gin rummy is a favourite tournament game, with players ranked according to ability. The top competition, the Gin Rummy Tournament of Champions, has annual prize money of over $50,000.

Number of players: Two.

Cards: One normal pack is used, with Aces counting low.

The deal: Each player is dealt ten cards. The remainder of the pack forms a stock pile, the top card of which is turned over to form the base of a discard pile. The top card of the discard pile is known as the *upcard*.

The start: The non-dealer has the option of taking the upcard. If he refuses, the dealer has the same option. If both refuse to take it, the non-dealer must start the game by drawing the top card from stock.

The play: Each player in turn draws a card, then discards one on the discard pile. It is not permissable for a player to draw the upcard and discard it in the same turn.

Players do not have the option of placing melded cards on the table, as in standard Seven-card rummy. Everything is held in hand.

The hand ends in one of two ways:

1   If a player can meld all his cards, he shows his hand and receives bonus points. This is known as *going gin*.
2   If the sum of the unmelded cards in a player's hand, known as the *deadwood*, is less than ten points, he can *knock*. He then lays down his hand, grouping the cards into melds and deadwood.

When either of these situations arises, the second player can lay down his own hand, with cards melded where possible.

If the first player has knocked, the second can add to the first player's melds. If the first has gone gin, the second can lay down only his own melded cards.

In both cases, the second player must count up the value of his deadwood, with all court cards counting ten.

The scoring: If a player has gone gin, he scores a bonus of twenty-five points, plus the value of his opponent's deadwood.

If a player has knocked, and his deadwood count is lower than his opponent, his score is the difference between the two deadwood counts.

If a player has knocked, but his opponent's deadwood count after laying off his cards is the same or lower, then the opponent is awarded a twenty-five-point bonus in addition to the difference in deadwood counts.

The game ends when either player reaches 100 points. The player who has reached the target is given a bonus of a further 100 points, plus twenty-five points for each individual hand he has won. If he has won every hand, the points are doubled up.

Strategy: The elements of observation and inference which were mentioned in relation to Seven-card rummy are equally applicable to Gin rummy.

An additional strategic factor is when to knock. It can be tempting, if you hold a promising hand, to go for gin. More often than not it does not work, and the chance of a high-scoring knock is lost. A typical game might use up half to two-thirds of the stock, so if you are in a position to knock much earlier than this, it will probably be worth your while.

If you are in any doubt about whether to take the upcard, then don't. The less your opponent knows about the contents of your hand, the more difficult it is for him to plan his play.

The American author D. L. Coburn immortalized Gin rummy in his award-winning play *The Gin Game*, which features two characters meeting and getting to know each other over a game of Gin rummy. As the author himself says, the game 'becomes the binding agent that at once brings them together, and serves as a catalyst for conflict that repeatedly tears them apart.'

One of the most interesting aspects of the play is that the performers have to change their lines according to the cards they pick up – but within limits; it is not unusual for one of the players to want a particular card, but be unable to pick it up as the script won't let him!

Everyone wants to die happy. Bing Crosby died playing golf, his favourite game. So too did Al Jolson, who expired during a game of Gin rummy on 23 October 1950.

Kalooki

This is a double-pack form of Rummy which is popular in such diverse locations as the card rooms of New York and the subways of Great Britain, where it is a favourite game amongst the staff of the London Underground system.

Number of players: Two to six, playing as individuals.

Cards: Two packs including four Jokers, making a total of 108 cards. Jokers are wild. All cards are valued, Aces at eleven points, other cards at face value. Jokers are valued according to their use within a meld – if a Joker is being used instead of 5C, it would be worth five points.

The cut: The player to the dealer's rights cuts the pack, and looks at the bottom of the cut portion. If the exposed card is a Joker, he takes it as his first card, otherwise he simply leaves it in position and completes the cut.

The deal: Fifteen cards are dealt to each player. If the Joker has been cut and taken, its recipient is omitted from the first round of the deal. The remainder of the pack forms a stock pile, with the top card turned up (the *upcard*) to start a discard pile.

The play: The dealer can choose to take the upcard. If so, he discards a card from his hand. If he declines the upcard, play passes to the player on the dealer's left, and clockwise thereafter.

Succeeding players can only take the upcard if they can meld it immediately, otherwise they must draw the top card from stock. An initial meld must be worth at least fifty-one points, based on the card values, although this can include cards laid off to other players' melds.

A Joker within a meld can be exchanged for the natural card it represents. For example, if a sequence reads 10S, Joker, QS, a player holding JS can, in his turn, exchange it for the Joker.

Melds can be made up of sets of the same rank, or sequences in the same suit.

The objective is to get rid of all your cards; if this is done in a single move, the player is said to have *gone kalooki*. If it is done over several turns, he has *gone rummy*.

Scoring: Each player must pay the winner one unit for each card held. If the winner has gone kalooki, the payments are doubled. If preferred, settlements can be made according to card values.

Two forms of Rummy which employ a similar feature of specific meld-building are Contract rummy and Progressive rummy.

Contract Rummy

Number of players: Two to eight.

Cards: Two normal packs, with 2s wild. Cards are valued as follows: A, 2, 3, 4, 5, 6, 7 are worth five points, 8, 9, 10, J, Q, K are worth ten points.

The deal: Each player is dealt ten cards. The remainder form a stock pile, the top card of which starts a discard pile.

The objective: Six hands are played, with specific melds having to be constructed on each hand.

   A *high group* comprises three ten-point cards of the same rank, for example JS, JH, JC.

   A *low group* comprises three five-point cards of the same rank, for example 6C, 6S, 6D.

   A *red sequence* is a sequence of hearts or diamonds.

   A *black sequence* is a sequence of clubs or spades.

   At any stage, a 2 can represent any card.

   The requirements for each hand are as follows:

1   One high and one low group.
2   One red and one black sequence.
3   One high group and one red sequence.
4   One low group and one black sequence.
5   Three sequences.
6   Three groups.

The play: The rules for drawing, melding and discarding are as for standard Seven-card rummy.

   The hand ends when a player has made the prescribed melds and got rid of all his cards.

   If the stock is exhausted before anyone has gone out, the upcard is removed to start a new discard pile, whilst the remainder of the old discard pile is shuffled and placed face-down as new stock.

The scoring: The winner of a hand is awarded points for each of the cards held by his opponents, according to the card point values. The losers have the points held deducted.

   The overall winner is the higher scorer after the six hands.

Progressive Rummy
The number of players, cards and deal are identical to Contract rummy. However, there are seven hands, with the requirements becoming progressively more difficult.

1 A three-card group or sequence.
2 A four-card group or sequence.
3 A five-card set or sequence.
4 Two three-card sets or sequences (or one of each).
5 A three and a four.
6 A three and a five.
7 Two fours.

A player must place the minimum requirement for the hand on the table as his initial meld. Then it is a matter of going out first.

Duplicate cards are not permitted within groups. In other words, a three-card group must have cards of three different suits; a four-card group must have all suits represented.

Scoring is based on face-values, with all court cards counting ten. Ace counts eleven, and can be used high or low in sequences.

Canasta

The most complex of the regularly played Rummy games, Canasta was invented in Uruguay in the 1940s, where its name means *basket*. Forming a canasta, the highest scoring combination in the game, could perhaps be likened to weaving a basket.

Number of players: Four, in two partnerships.

Cards: Two packs are used, with the four Jokers included, making a total of 108 cards. Twelve of these are wild cards, the four Jokers and the eight 2s. They can represent any card.

All cards have values, which are required for melding and scoring. The values are:

Joker	50 points
Aces and 2s	20 points
High cards (K, Q, J, 10, 9, 8)	10 points
Low cards (7, 6, 5, 4 and black 3)	5 points
Red 3	100 points

The deal: Eleven cards are dealt to each player. The rest of the cards form a stock pile, the top card of which is turned up to form the base of a discard pile, generally referred to as *the pack*. The top card of the pack is known as the *upcard*. If it is a Joker, a 2 or a red 3, a second card must be turned up, and so on until the upcard is anything other than one of the three cards mentioned.

At this point all players holding red 3s must place them on the table, replenishing their hands from stock. When everyone's hand has been restored to eleven cards, play can commence.

The play: As in standard Rummy, each player's turn comprises three elements: draw, meld and discard.

A player must first draw, either the top card from stock or, subject to certain restrictions, the whole of the pack.

If a card drawn from stock is a red 3, it is placed on the table in front of the player, and a second card is drawn.

The pack can only be picked up if the upcard is immediately meldable, either laid off to an existing meld, or used to complete a meld within a player's hand. A new meld must contain at least two *natural*, as opposed to wild cards.

If the pack is *frozen*, then it can only be picked up by a player who can form a new, natural meld of three or more cards, including the upcard. This automatically unfreezes the pack. There are three ways in which the pack can become frozen:

1   It is frozen to a partnership which has yet to lay down its first meld.
2   It is frozen to everyone if it contains a wild card or a red 3. The latter case can only occur if the red 3 has been turned up initially.
3   It is frozen for the duration of the next player's turn if a black 3 is discarded.

Having drawn, a player can form or add to melds. These must comprise cards of the same rank, with each meld containing at least two natural cards, and no more than three wild cards.

A meld of seven or more cards is known as a *canasta*. If there are no wild cards it is a *natural canasta*, and must be topped with a red card. Otherwise it is a *mixed canasta*, and should be topped with a black card.

Melds are held by a partnership, so a player can, in his turn, add to melds formed by his partner.

Red 3s are never melded, and black 3s can only be melded on the turn that a player goes out.

A partnership cannot lay down its first meld unless its value meets an initial points requirement, which varies according to the state of the game. Initial meld requirements are as follows:

Current score	Required value
A minus figure	15 points
0–1500	50 points
1500–3000	90 points
3000–5000	120 points

For example, if a partnership is unfortunate enough to have a minus score, a meld of three 4s will be sufficient to get it on its way. On the other hand, a partnership with 4000 points would need something like KS, KH, KD, 2H, 2C, Joker (woth 120 points) to get started.

Although the pack is frozen until a side has made its first meld, the pack can be taken if the upcard will combine to form a meld of sufficient value to satisfy the initial requirement.

Having melded where possible (or desired) the player discards one card. A red 3 cannot be discarded, although any other card can. A black 3 will freeze the pack for the left-hand opponent, whilst a wild card will freeze it for everyone.

The hand ends when either member of a partnership goes out. A player cannot go out unless his side has formed at least one canasta. It is customary for a player who is in a position to go out to ask his partner's permission. If the reply is 'No!' he is bound by it.

A player who goes out without previously having melded any cards is said to have *gone out blind*.

The scoring: Bonus points are scored as follows:

Going out	100 points
Going out blind	200 points
Natural canasta	500 points
Mixed canasta	300 points
Each red 3	100 points
All four red 3s	800 points

In addition, the card values of every card on the table are totalled up. This gives a partnership its plus score on the deal. The values of any cards still held in hand are deducted to give the overall score.

If a side has failed to meld any cards when the opposition goes out, any red 3s become penalty cards and take a value of -100 points.

It is quite normal for the side going out to score less than their opponents.

The first side to reach 5000 points wins.

Strategy: Unlike most Rummy games, the main objective in Canasta is not to go out quickly. It is to accumulate points, and the more points you and your partner are accumulating, the less reason there is to go out.

The method of building up points revolves around capturing the discard pile, the pack. Every time you capture the pack it gives you a new selection of cards for melding. And the more cards that you hold, the easier it is to recapture the pack.

Making an initial meld is very important, so that the pack is unfrozen for you and your partner. Try to do this as economically as possible; the more cards that are held in your hand, the less information your opponents will have about discarding.

145

Probably the best time to start wide-scale melding is after capturing a large discard pile. Your opponents will have a fair idea of the contents of your hand, so the cards might as well be out on the table.

Canasta is a game where the side gaining an early initiative is immediately in a strong position. Success breeds success. Therefore there are many situations where your strategy must be defensive rather than offensive.

Freezing the pack is an important defensive measure. If your opponents have started well, it may prevent them capturing a lucrative pack.

Try to discard low cards early on. Obviously it is more difficult to build initial melds with cards valued at five points rather than ten. If you must throw cards which are likely to be helpful to your opponents, do it while the pack is small, or, better still, frozen.

Although going out is not the principal aim, there are certain situations where it is necessary. If your opponents have started well, it can be a means of cutting losses. Alternatively, if your partnership has taken an early initiative but your opponents appear to be catching up, this might be a good time to go out and accept a small profit. Finally, if your opponents have melded few but are holding many cards, go out if you can – there's nothing more humiliating than being caught with a handful.

Although small amounts of money might change hands in most Rummy games, there were no true gambling games in the family until the 1930s. Two variations which do involve high stakes are *Banking Rummy* and *Pif Paf*.

Banking Rummy

Invented in 1935 by Harry J. Dorey, Banking rummy is essentially standard Six-card rummy with betting beforehand.

One player is banker, and must handle all bets.

Before the cards are dealt, the players are able to make two different types of bet:

1   **Bet on spades** – each player can bet any amount within the house limit, that their highest spade will be higher than the banker's highest spade. The player must also add a five per cent charge for making the bet. For example, if a player bets £1, he must pay an additional 5p. If the player wins the bet, he receives £1 from the banker in addition to his initial stake of £1.

2   **Bet on specific cards** – each player can bet on the specific rank and suit of two cards in his first six dealt. Usually only pairs are called, to make the banker's job a little easier. If the two cards selected appear in the player's hand, the banker pays out 70 times the amount of the bet. The maximum bet must be set according to the funds of the banker. The actual odds on guessing two cards correctly are 87.4 to 1 against, so the banker does stand to make a reasonable return.

Once betting has been concluded, play continues as in the normal Six-card rummy.

Pif-Paf

The betting in Pif-Paf is similar to that of games such as Poker and Brag. The play is similar to Rummy.

Number of players: Four to eight.

Cards: Two normal packs are used.

The deal: Each player is dealt nine cards.

Objective: To get rid of all one's cards by melding them in groups and sequences, and thus win the pot.

The betting: All players place one chip in the pot. The dealer places one chip in the pot for each player. Therefore if there were six players there would be eleven chips in the pot, six from the dealer and one from each of the other players.

The player to the dealer's left starts the betting. He has the choice of raising blind, or looking at his hand and matching the dealer's initial contribution. If he does raise blind, his bet must be double the dealer's amount.

The other players may look at their hands, or continue to raise blind, doubling the amount each time. Having looked at their hands, players have the choice of staying in the game or dropping out. If they decide to stay in, they must 'equalize' their bets with the blind player. For example, if Player one has bet 12 blind, and Player two has raised to 24, then if Player three looked at his hand and wished to stay in, he would have to bet 24 also. If the betting then came back round to Player one, he would have to bet another 12 chips to bring his total contribution up to 24.

The amounts can continue to rise on each round of betting, until eventually no one wishes to raise further, and all bets have been equalized.

Play can then start, with the top card turned up and the player to the dealer's left going first. Play follows the standard Rummy rules, except that if a player needs the top card of the discard pile to go out, he can take it *'out of turn'* – he then must go out immediately, otherwise he is out of the game.

The first player to go out wins the pot.

The Hearts Family

If you always seem to hold lousy cards, then Hearts and its many variants could be the answer – because success in Hearts depends not on winning tricks, but on avoiding winning them!

Standard Hearts

Number of players: Three to seven.

Cards: Normal pack used. If there are three players, one of the four 2s should be discarded. For five players, two 2s are discarded, for seven players three 2s. THE 2H SHOULD NEVER BE DISCARDED.

The deal: All cards are dealt, an equal number to each player.

The play: The player to the dealer's left leads to the first trick, thereafter the player winning the previous trick leads. A player must follow suit where possible, otherwise he discards. There are no trumps. The highest card in the suit led wins the trick. The hand finishes when all cards have been played.

  If a player fails to follow suit when he is able to, and does not notice his mistake before the trick is picked up, the hand ends and he scores thirteen penalty points.

The scoring: One penalty point is scored for each card in the hearts suit held in tricks won. For example, if you have won a trick containing 3H, 7H, QH and 9C your opponent is awarded three points.

Strategy: It is best to win tricks early with high cards, so that other players cannot discard their hearts later on. It is always useful to have low cards to lead out. Leading a short suit is good tactics, as this may provide the opportunity to discard hearts on the suit at a later stage.

Sample Hand – Standard Hearts

There are five players, Ann, Brian, Colin, Debbie and Eugene. Henceforth they will be referred to as A, B, C, D and E.

  With five players, two 2s must be discarded, excluding the 2H. The players elect to discard 2D and 2C.

  Ann deals the cards as follows:

	A	B	C	D	E
Spades	A, 5, 2	K, 10	8, 6, 3	J, 9	Q, 7, 4
Hearts	4, 3	A, K, 6, 2	9, 8	Q, 7, 5	J, 10
Diamonds	A, Q, 6	7, 4, 3	K, 5	10	J, 9, 8
Clubs	K, 8	Q	10, 9, 4	A, 7, 6, 3	J, 5

  Ann's left-hand opponent, Brian, leads to the first trick. He chooses to lead his short suit, clubs.

Trick 1: B leads QC, C plays 10C, D plays AC, E plays JC, A plays KC. Note that each player has played the highest available card in the suit. Debbie has won the trick, so she leads to Trick 2.

Trick 2: D leads 10D, E plays JD, A plays AD, B plays 7D, C plays KD. Ann now decides to gamble on a second round of diamonds, in the hope that they are evenly distributed. . . .

Trick 3: A leads QD, B plays 3D, C plays 5D, D plays QH, E plays 9D. So Debbie has been able to ditch one of her hearts. Ann is still on lead, but now has one penalty point.

Trick 4: A leads AS, B plays KS, C plays 8S, D plays JS, E plays QS. Once again it is Ann to lead. She now decides to lead a small heart, knowing it cannot win the trick.

Trick 5: A leads 3H, B plays 6H, C plays 9H, D plays 7H, E plays JH. This is bad news for Eugene, who has just picked up five penalty points. He decides to lead a low club.

Trick 6: E leads 5C, A plays 8C, B plays AH, C plays 4C, D plays 6C. Yet again Ann has won the trick, and one of her opponents, in this case Brian, has been able to ditch a heart, so Ann now has two penalty points. She decides to lead her second small heart.

Trick 7: A leads 4H, B plays 2H, C plays 8H, D plays 5H, E plays 10H. Another five penalty points for Eugene! He chooses to lead a small spade.

Trick 8: E leads 4S, A plays 5S, B plays 10S, C plays 6S, D plays 9S. Brian has won his first trick, and with no hearts discarded. He now leads the 4D.

Trick 9: B leads 4D, C plays 9C, D play 7C, E plays 8D, A plays 6D. Eugene must now lead to the final trick.

Trick 10: E leads 7S, A plays 2S, B plays KH, C plays 3S, D plays 3C. So Eugene has won the final trick, and picked up another heart in the bargain!

The scoring: Eugene has picked up five penalty points twice, in tricks 5 and 7. In addition, the KH was discarded on the final trick. Therefore he has a total of $5 + 5 + 1 = 11$ penalty points.

The other two hearts were discarded on tricks 3 and 6, both of which were won by Ann. So she has $1 + 1 = 2$ penalty points.

The other three players, Brian, Colin and Debbie, have no penalties.

It is interesting to note that Brian, who appeared to have the most awkward hand, with four hearts including the top two, ended up being able to discard in such a way that he didn't win any tricks in hearts.

The hand also shows that it is often the 'middle' cards, the 9s and 10s, which prove to be the most destructive.

Although the basic game of Hearts gives scope for both skill and ingenuity, its early devotees soon began to look around for something a little more exciting. Gradually, a number of variants on the original game developed.

The first involved each player, after looking at his hand, passing three selected cards to the player on his right. These would have to be passed on before the three cards received were looked at.

The second involved the introduction of new penalty cards, notably the Queen of spades. She soon became known by a number of highly uncomplimentary nicknames, ranging from 'The Black Lady' to 'The Slippery Bitch'. Nowadays, almost all forms of Hearts use the Queen of spades as the ultimate card to avoid. In most versions she counts for thirteen penalty points, as many as the whole of the heart suit put together!

Changes in the system of scoring were also tried. In **Spot hearts** the play is identical to the basic game, but each card in the heart suit is counted at its face value, with the King counting thirteen, the Queen twelve and the Jack eleven.

Many versions of the game incorporate a clause in the scoring system whereby if a player takes *all* the penalty cards, each of his opponents receives 150 penalty points.

Greek hearts employs all three variations, an initial card-exchange, the Queen of spades as a penalty card, and the Spot system of scoring, with the additional stipulation that the Queen of hearts is worth fifty penalty points.

Black Maria, one of the most popular versions, uses the original method of scoring, but features initial card-exchange and has three penalty cards in the spade suit – the Ace (seven points), the King (ten points) and the Queen, or 'Black Maria' (thirteen points).

I particularly enjoy the game **Joker hearts**. This employs the 'spanner in the works' principle, with one card in the pack designed to wreak havoc when it appears.

Joker Hearts
Number of players: Three to seven
Cards: Normal pack, except that the 2H is discarded, and replaced with a Joker. Additional cards are discarded according to the number of players, as in Standard Hearts.
The deal: All cards are dealt, an equal number to each player.
The play: This is identical to Standard Hearts, except for the misdemeanours of the Joker. It ranks between the 10 and Jack of hearts, and wins *any* trick in which it is played, regardless of the suit led. Unless, that is, a higher heart is also played in the trick, in which case the higher heart wins.
   The player holding the Joker must follow suit if hearts are led.
The scoring: Each heart counts one penalty point, except for the Joker which is worth five.

So far it has seemed that the Hearts family has been spawned by those of a somewhat morbid disposition, with nothing but 'bad' cards and penalty points. It's nice to know that there are also variations where plus points are awarded.

In **Omnibus hearts** the 10 of diamonds provides a ten-point bonus for the player winning the trick containing it. **Red jack hearts** is identical, except that the bonus card is the Jack of diamonds.

Some of the more interesting members of the Hearts family feature characteristics of better-known games.

Auction Hearts

This is a gambling game, where players bid to set the suit of penalty cards.

Number of players: Three to seven.

Cards: Normal pack used, but with 2s discarded according to the number of players, as in Standard Hearts.

The deal: All cards are dealt, an equal number to each player.

The bidding: Each player, in turn, makes a bid to name the suit of penalty cards. If he is not prepared to bid higher than the previous player, he passes. The bid is in the form of chips, or whatever is being used as units of play. The highest bidder has the right to name the suit, but it is only when the bidding is complete that he announces it, after placing the number of chips bid into the pot.

The play: The successful bidder leads. Once all cards have been played out, in the usual fashion, each player counts up the number of penalty cards in the tricks he has won.

Settlement: Each player places one chip in the pot for each penalty card he holds. The player with no penalty card takes the pot. If two players have no penalty cards, the pot is shared. But if more than two players have no penalty cards, or if each player has at least one, no one wins, and play continues with the successful bidder from the previous hand again choosing the penalty suit. In this way the pot can gradually accumulate. When it is finally won, bidding recommences on the next hand.

For card players who are used to bidding for trumps in games such as Bridge, Auction hearts introduces a whole new dimension, where the idea is to bid your weakest suits, in the hope of not taking tricks!

Domino Hearts

Number of players: Two to seven.

Cards: Normal pack used.

The deal: Six cards are dealt to each player. The remainder form a stock from which cards can be drawn.

The play: As normal, except that if a player cannot follow suit, he must draw cards from the stock pile until he is able to do so. Once the stock is exhausted discarding occurs in the usual way. As a player uses his last card, he drops out for the remainder of the hand. Where a player wins a trick with his last active card, the player on his left leads to the following trick. Play ends when only one player is left in.

The scoring: One penalty point is scored for each heart in tricks won. The last player left in also scores penalty points for any hearts remaining in his hand, or in the stock pile. If the final players have gone out simultaneously, the last to play a card has the stock scored against him.

Once one of the players reaches thirty-one penalty points, the player with the lowest number of penalty points wins.

Draw Hearts

Number of players: Two.

Cards: Normal pack used.

The deal: Thirteen cards are dealt to each player. The remainder form a stock from which cards can be drawn.

The play: After each trick, both players draw a card from the stock, winner first. Thus each player's hand is maintained at thirteen cards until the stock is exhausted, at which point the remaining cards are simply played out.

The scoring: Each player counts up the number of hearts in his tricks. The player with fewer hearts is awarded points corresponding to the difference. For example, if one player has five hearts and the other has eight, the first scores $8 - 5 = 3$ points. Most games are played up to 50 or 100 points.

One or two of the more unusual Hearts games are played with 'the Piquet pack', which contains only thirty-two cards, with nothing lower than a 7.

Polignac
Also known as **Four Jacks**, this is the French form of Hearts.
Number of players: Three to seven.
Cards: The 32-card Piquet pack is used. Depending on the number of players, the 7s are discarded so that the deck can be dealt out evenly. The 7H should *not* be discarded.
The deal: The cards are dealt out two at a time, to each player in rotation.
The play: The object is to avoid winning tricks containing Jacks; however, a player may, before the opening lead, declare his intention to win all the tricks. If he is successful, each of his opponents receive five penalty points. If he fails, he receives five penalty points. The play itself is as in Standard Hearts.
The scoring: Each Jack held in tricks taken counts one penalty point, except for the Jack of spades, or *Polignac*, which counts two. Generally a game will be set at ten points. As soon as one player reaches it, the player with the lowest score is the winner.

155

Slobberhannes
The splendidly named Slobberhannes uses the same pack, the same deal and the same method of play as Polignac, but here the object is to avoid winning the first trick, the last trick and the trick containing the Queen of clubs.

A penalty point is scored for each, and if a player has the misfortune to win all three tricks he is rewarded with an extra penalty point.

The game is usually set at ten points, as with Polignac.

Knaves

The game Knaves is really something of a hybrid. It combines the rewards for trick-taking associated with the Whist family with the penalties for certain cards associated with Hearts. As such, it provides the opportunity for a high level of skill to be used; the need to avoid winning certain tricks, while striving to win others.

Number of players: Three.

Cards: Normal pack used.

The deal: Seventeen cards are dealt to each player. The remaining one is turned up, and sets the trump suit.

The play: The player to the dealer's left leads to the first trick; thereafter the player winning the previous trick leads. The objective is to win as many tricks as possible, but to avoid winning tricks containing a Jack. Players must follow suit if possible, otherwise they can trump or discard. The hand finishes when all cards have been played.

The scoring: One point is scored for each trick taken, but penalty points are deducted for those containing Jacks, four points for JH, three points for JD, two points for JC and one point for JS. The first player to obtain twenty points is the winner.

Strategy: Although each player plays for himself, it is possible for two to team up if the third is getting too far ahead. In Knaves, it is possible to pull anyone down to your level!

One of the joys of the Hearts family is that it is so easy to invent your own game – one or two new penalty cards, a change in the scoring – anything is possible!

The Stops Family

There appears to be no strong historical element in the development of the family known as Stops games. There is merely a common factor amidst a varied selection – namely that when a player does not hold the right card or cards to continue play, he is *stopped* and play passes to the next player.

It is the same principle as that used in dominoes. In fact one of the Stops games, Fan Tan, is alternatively known as Card dominoes. However, it is not the most popular game in the family. That honour belongs to Newmarket, so named because much of the pleasure lies in the betting.

Newmarket

Alternatively known as **Michigan** or **Boodle**, this is a simple game but one which rewards skill and flair.

Number of players: Three to eight.

Cards: One normal pack is used. In addition an Ace, King, Queen and Jack, each of a different suit, are removed from a second pack and placed in the centre of the table. These are known as the *boodle cards*.

Betting: Before each deal, all players must place bets, with a previously agreed number of chips being staked, usually ten. The bets are placed on the four boodle cards.

Objectives: To play cards corresponding to the boodle cards, thus winning the chips placed on them; to be the first to get rid of all cards.

The deal: All cards are dealt in a clockwise motion, but as though there were an extra player. Thus if there are five players, six hands are dealt. Leftover cards are put aside.

Exchanging: After looking at his hand, the dealer has the option to exchange it for the extra one dealt. If he chooses to do so, his old hand is placed face down on the table. If the dealer chooses not to exchange, he auctions off the right to the other players. The highest bidder pays the dealer the number of chips bid, then carries out the exchange.

The play: The player to the dealer's left leads the lowest card in one of his suits. Play then continues with the next card up being played by whoever holds it, until a situation is reached where no continuation is possible, either because the Ace has been played, or because the next card in sequence is in the waste hand. This is a *Stop* situation.

When a Stop occurs, the player who has played the last card now leads the lowest in another suit. If he does not have another suit, play passes to the player on his left.

As cards are played, they are placed in a pile in front of each player, and cannot be looked at.

When a card is played corresponding to a boodle card, the player who has played it collects all the chips placed on the boodle card. If the corresponding card does not appear – it could be in the waste hand or the player holding it has been unable to play it – the chips remain on the boodle card for the following deal, although bets are placed just as before.

Play ends when one player uses up all his cards. He is then paid by the other players, one chip for each card they still hold.

If a player is shown to have played incorrectly, he must pay each of his opponents one chip compensation; if his incorrect play has prevented someone winning a boodle bonus, he must pay the number of chips on the boodle card.

Strategy: Whether or not to bid for the exchange hand depends on whether a boodle-corresponding card is held. Bear in mind that if you bid successfully, and get the exchange hand, you will have gained an advantage, since you will be the only player to know the contents of the concealed hand.

Always lead the suit in which you hold a boodle card at every opportunity.

Sample Hand – Newmarket

There are four players, Adrian, Betty, Charles and Diana, also known as A, B, C and D.

The four boodle cards are AS, KH, QD and JC.

The players have agreed to stake ten chips on each hand. Adrian bets three chips on AS and KH, two chips on QD and JC. Betty does the reverse, three chips on QD and JC, two on AS and KH. Charles gambles – he bets all ten on QD. Diana puts five chips on KH and five on QD.

So the total amount on the boodle cards is as follows:

Ace of spades	$3 + 2 = 5$
King of hearts	$3 + 2 + 5 = 10$
Queen of diamonds	$2 + 3 + 10 + 5 = 20$
Jack of clubs	$2 + 3 = 5$

Adrian deals as follows:

	A	B	C	D	Extra
Spades	Q, 10, 9, 7	8, 6	A, 3, 2	K, 4	J, 5
Hearts	–	A, Q, J, 9, 8	10, 7	K, 6, 3, 2	–
Diamonds	9, 6, 5	8	Q, J	10, 2	A, K, 7, 4, 3
Clubs	Q, 10, 2	4, 3	K, J, 9	A, 5	8, 7, 6

5H and 4H are left out.

Adrian decides that his hand is not much use. There is nothing corresponding to the boodle cards, and he will be stuck if hearts are led. Therefore he elects to exchange, after mentally noting the contents of his old hand.

Betty leads off, and since she has no boodle cards she decides to play her longest suit, in the hope of clearing her hand quickly.

Round 1: B plays 8H, 9H. C plays 10H. B plays JH, QH. D plays KH, and claims the ten chips placed on it. B plays AH. STOP.

Round 2: B plays 3C, 4C. D plays 5C. A plays 6C, 7C, 8C (remember he now has what was the extra hand). C plays 9C. STOP.

Round 3: C plays JD, QD and claims the twenty chips – his bet has come off! A plays KD, AD. STOP.

Round 4: A plays 3D, 4D. STOP. 5D and 6D are in the waste hand.

Round 5: A plays 7D. A bad decision! He has let in Betty. B plays 8D. STOP.

Round 6: B plays 6S. STOP.

Round 7: B plays 8S.

Betty is now out of cards, so the game ends. The players must all count up how many cards they have left.

Adrian holds two, JS and 5S, so he pays Betty two chips.

Charles holds six, AS, 3S, 2S, 7H, KC, JC. He has been unable to claim on

two boodle cards, AS and JC, but the twenty chips won on QD more than compensate for it. He pays Betty six chips.

Diana has done badly. She still holds eight cards, KS, 4S, 6H, 3H, 2H, 10D, 2D, AC, but at least she has won ten chips on KH. She pays Betty eight chips.

The overall situation is as follows:

Adrian   10 bid + 2 paid = 12 loss.
Betty   10 bid and (2 + 6 + 8) = 16 received, gives 6 profit.
Charles   10 bid and 20 received gives 10 profit.
Diana   10 bid and 10 received – no change.

The five chips on AS and JC will remain for the following hand.

There are numerous variations on the basic game of Newmarket.

A simplified version removes the hand-exchange stage, although an extra hand is still dealt to provide the Stop cards; it simply remains unseen throughout the play.

A second variant demands a standard stake, usually one chip, to be placed on each of the boodle cards by all the players.

In **Cross-colour Michigan** a player can only lead a suit of the opposite colour to the last one played.

In **Spinade**, a player can stop any sequence by playing the Ace of diamonds, and announcing 'Spin'. He is then free to lead the lowest card in a new suit. The Ace of diamonds can only be played when it is legitimately the player's turn, in other words, immediately after he has played an eligible card in the correct sequence.

Pope Joan, which is reputed to be a forerunner of Newmarket itself, has specific boodle cards: the 9 and 10 of diamonds, the Jack of clubs, the Queen of spades and the King of hearts. Only the dealer places chips on the cards, one on the 10, two on the Jack, three on the Queen, four on the King and five on the 9. At the end of the hand, if a player is caught with a card corresponding to one of the boodle cards, he must double the stake before the next hand is dealt. Needless to say, the deal must rotate from player to player.

Fan Tan

This is the card player's version of dominoes. It is also a game which can totally change your perspective regarding 'good' and 'bad' hands. In Fan Tan, high cards or low cards spell trouble; a decent smattering of 6s, 7s and 8s should make your eyes light up.

Number of players: Two to eight.

Cards: One normal pack is used.

Stakes: Each player must place one chip in a pot before the deal.

The deal: All the cards are dealt out. If they come out unevenly, those with fewer cards must place another chip in the pot.

The play: The player to the dealer's left leads any 7. If he does not have one, he contributes another chip and play passes to his left. Whenever anyone cannot play, he must pay a chip into the pot. Eventually a 7 is played, say 7C. The next player can now play another 7 above or below the first, or 6C to the left or 8C to the right.

In this way sequences are built up to the Kings on the right, and to the Aces, which count low in this game, to the left.

The hand ends as soon as one player uses up all his cards. He is then paid one unit for each card held by the other players.

If a player fails to play when he could have done, he must pay three chips into the pot.

Strategy: It is best to retain 7s if at all possible, as they can be played at any time. Try to move the sequences towards your own high or low cards.

161

Comet

The return of Halley's comet in 1759 proved to be the inspiration for this game, which is the oldest known member of the Stops family.

Number of players: Two to five.

Cards: Two identical packs are required. The Aces are removed, then all the black cards are used as one pack, and all the red cards as the other. Finally, one of the club 9s is placed in the red pack, and one of the diamond 9s is placed in the black pack.

The deal: Cards are dealt in a clockwise motion, but some are held back to form a 'dead' hand containing Stop cards. The number of undealt cards varies according to the number of players. For two or three players, twelve cards are left undealt, for four players eight cards, and for five players three cards. The red and black packs are used for alternate deals.

The play: The player to the dealer's left leads any card. He then continues to play cards in ascending sequence, regardless of suit. When he has no eligible card, play passes to the player on his left. When the King is reached, or the next eligible card is in the dead hand, the player who has created the stop situation leads any card to restart play.

More than one card of a particular rank can be played in a turn. For example, if 9C is the last card played, the next player could get rid of all the 10s he possesses in one move.

The odd-coloured 9, or *comet*, is a wild card which can be played at any time, in lieu of any card.

The game ends as soon as one player uses all his cards.

The scoring: The winner is paid one chip for each card held by his opponents. If the comet has not been played, its holder must pay double.

Eights

Also known as **Crazy eights** or **Swedish rummy**, this is an exciting and fast-moving game which is particularly well-suited as a family game – easy to learn for children, entertaining for adults.

Number of players: Two to eight.

Cards: For two to four players, one normal pack is used. For more than four players, two packs are shuffled together.

The deal: Each player is dealt five cards. The top card of stock is turned up and placed in the centre of the table as a *starter*, unless it is an 8 in which case it is put back in the centre of the pack and a second card is turned over.

The play: The player to the dealer's left plays first. We must play a card of the same suit or the same rank as the starter. For example, if the starter is 9H, he must play either a heart, or another 9.

The 8s are wild cards, and can be played at any time regardless of suit or rank. The player producing the 8 has the option of naming a new suit.

Play rotates clockwise around the table, with each player contributing one card per move. If a player has no eligible card he must pick from stock until he can play, or until the stock is exhausted.

The first player to get rid of all his cards wins the hand. If a blocked situation occurs where no one can play, the player with the lowest point count in his hand wins, where an 8 counts for fifty points, King, Queen, Jack and 10 count ten, and other cards score their face values.

The losing players must pay the winner an amount equivalent to the point-count in their hands, although scores can be kept on paper rather than in the form of chips.

Strategy: 8s are obviously the most valuable cards. They should only be played where no other card is useable. It is good tactics to play long suits, so as to force opponents to pick from stock.

Eights is a game which is particularly susceptible to variations and mutations of all types.

In **Wild Jacks**, the Jacks are wild cards instead of the 8s, whereas in **Go boom** there are no wild cards whatsoever, so the suit can only be changed when a card of the same rank is played.

I once played a game which is a hybrid of Eights and the old children's game of Beggar my neighbour. I have been unable to trace it in card literature, so I shall call it **Switch**, since it involves switching both suit and direction.

Switch

Number of players: Two to eight.

Cards: One normal pack is used for two to four players. For five or more players, two packs are used.

The deal: Five cards are dealt to each player, with the top card of stock turned up as a starter.

The play: This is essentially the same as in Eights, with play initially rotating in a clockwise direction, and with players having to follow either with the same suit or rank. However, in the event of someone being unable to play, they would take only one card, except in the situations described below, before play moved on to the next player. A player cannot pick and play in one round. There are no wild cards, although particular cards, when eligible for play, have certain attributes:

1 *A 5* switches the direction of play, from clockwise to anti-clockwise, or vice versa.

2 *An 8* 'skips' the next player, causing play to move instead to the next but one.

3 *A Jack* enables the player to change suits.

4 *A Queen* requires the next player to pick two cards. Only if he has a Queen himself can he play, in which case the following player must pick four cards, two for each Queen. If all four Queens appeared, the unfortunate player following this royal cavalcade would have to pick eight cards.

5 *A King* requires the next player to pick three cards. The same playing rules apply as for the Queen.

6 *An Ace* requires the next player to pick four cards; playing rules as for the King and Queen. Four successive Aces would force the next player to pick sixteen cards, if sufficient stock remained!

The winner is the first player to get rid of all his cards.

Enfle

This ancient Stops game incorporates the concept of trick-taking, even though the tricks themselves count for nothing.

Number of players: Four to six.

Cards: There should be eight cards per player. Thus for four players thirty-two cards are required, for five players forty cards, and for six players forty-eight. Unwanted cards are stripped out of the pack before play begins, the lowest (2s) first, then 3s, 4s and so on.

The deal: All (remaining) cards are dealt, eight to each player.

The play: The player to the dealer's left leads any card. The remaining players must follow suit if possible. Completed tricks are discarded on to a waste heap, with the winner of the trick leading to the next one.

If a player cannot follow suit, he must pick up and add to his hand the cards already played to the trick, before leading to the next one.

The first player to get rid of all his cards wins the hand.

Strategy: It is best to maintain a balance in one's hand, with cards from each suit. This is best achieved by leading from long suits.

Mau-Mau

A direct descendant of Eights, Mau-Mau is the newest documented game in the Stops family, believed to originate from New Zealand.

Number of players: Two.

Cards: One normal pack is used.

The deal: Each player is dealt seven cards. The remainder form a stock pile, the top card of which is turned up as a starter.

The play: Play passes alternately from player to player, starting with the non-dealer. Each card played must be of the same suit or rank as the top card of the heap built on the starter card. If a player has no eligible card, he must pick the top card from stock and add it to his hand. An eligible card *must* be played, otherwise a fifty-point penalty is imposed.

There are three special cards, which alter the normal run of play:

1   If one player plays a 7, his opponent must draw one card from stock, even if he could otherwise play.
2   If one player plays an 8, his opponent must draw three cards from stock, even if he could otherwise play.
3   Playing a Jack entitles the player to change the suit.

As soon as a player reduces his hand to a single card, he must announce 'One card'. If he fails to do so, he must pick from stock on his next turn, regardless of whether he could otherwise play out.

The hand ends when either player uses all his cards.

Scoring: The player who has used all his cards is awarded points according to the cards still held by his opponent. Jack and 8 score twenty points, 7 and Ace score fifteen points, King, Queen and 10 score ten points, and the remaining cards are scored at face value.

Normally a game is played up to 500 points.

Strategy: It is normally best to play one's long suit. It is good if 7s and 8s can be saved for the end of a hand, assuming you will not get stuck with them, because your opponent will be forced to draw cards which may count heavily against him.

The Patience Family

I remember, when I was young, being taught by my mother how to play Patience. No doubt I had been trying hers all morning, and she visualized a period of peace while I wrestled with the cards.

Some while later I discovered, to my delight, a second method of playing Patience, and was able to vary the two so as to avoid monotony.

Had I but known it, I could have played a different form of Patience every day for a year and still have had loads left over. There are more than five hundred documented Patience games, each demanding differing degrees of time, skill and luck.

The name Patience comes from the French, although it could equally well be English since the word has identical meanings in both languages. The earliest reference to the game itself comes from the Baltic area of Europe. It reached Britain in the 1870s, and was soon being very widely played. Perhaps Prince Albert's passion for Patience was a contributory factor in its spread; no doubt many devotees relished the fact that they were passing their leisure time in the same way as Queen Victoria's husband.

The objective in most Patience games is to transform a shuffled pack of cards into an ordered one. What makes each game different is the method in which the ordering takes place. In some cases, the lie of the cards is crucial; in others a skilled player can reach a successful conclusion regardless.

As befits its American name of **Solitaire**, Patience is generally a game for one player. However, there are competitive types of Patience, where two or more players enter battle armed only with their respective packs of cards.

The following selection includes examples of each and every variation: single-pack, double-pack, solitaire and competitive.

Single-Pack Patience Games

Generally, these require a little less time, less space and, with one or two exceptions, less sustained brain-power than their double-pack relatives.

They are Patience games for the impatient person!

Nevertheless, they still provide a stimulating and highly enjoyable way of passing idle moments. . . .

Sir Tommy

Also known as **Old patience**, this is reputed to be the forefather of all Patience games. As one might expect, it is very simple in concept; but getting it to come out is a different matter!

Cards: One normal pack is used.

Setting out: Deal the top four cards, face up. These form the four heaps referred to during play. If any are Aces, place them below to form foundations.

Objective: To build from the foundations in ascending order, regardless of suit, four piles topped by the four Kings.

The play: Turn over all the cards from the stock pile, one at a time. An Ace is immediately used as a foundation. Other cards are played as follows:

(a) If possible, a card is used to build from a foundation. This may allow other cards from the heaps to be similarly built.

(b) If building is not possible, the card must be placed on one of the heaps, at the player's discretion.

Strategy: The odds are stacked heavily against the player, but chances can be improved through judicious play. Try to avoid blocking low cards, and if possible balance the four heaps, one for high cards, one for low cards, and two somewhere in between.

Calculation

This is an unusual and entertaining variation on Sir Tommy. As its name implies, there is a greater logistical element involved.

Its objective is identical, to obtain four piles topped by the Kings, and the method of play is essentially the same; however, the starting point is quite different.

Setting out: Four cards should be selected from the pack, an Ace, a 2, a 3 and a 4. These are then laid down as foundations, but there are strict rules for building.

Building rules: Suit is unimportant, but the order of cards is different for each foundation:

1 *On the Ace*, cards must be built as follows: 2, 3, 4, 5, 6, 7, 8, 9, 10, J, Q, K.
2 *On the 2*, the order is: 4, 6, 8, 10, Q, A, 3, 5, 7, 9, J, K.
3 *On the 3*, the order is: 6, 9, Q, 2, 5, 8, J, A, 4, 7, 10, K.
4 *On the 4*, the order is: 8, Q, 3, 7, J, 2, 6, 10, A, 5, 9, K.

Thus the foundation card indicates the increment for building.

The play: The remainder of the pack, minus the four foundation cards, is shuffled and turned up, one card at a time. If a card cannot be built, it must be placed in one of four waste heaps which are created as the game progresses. At any stage, the top cards on the waste heaps can be built on to the foundations.

The game ends when the stock pile is exhausted. No redeal is allowed.

Strategy: Since the Kings are the last cards to be built, it would be foolish to place them over other cards in the waste heaps. It is perhaps best to reserve one heap for Kings only.

If possible, try to retain a situation where each of the foundations requires a different card for continuation.

Alternate

Another Sir Tommy variation, requiring two-way thinking.

Setting out: The two red Aces and the two black Kings are selected from the pack, and set out as foundations.

Building rules: The Aces are built from in ascending sequence and alternating colour, ending in the two red Kings. The black Kings are built from in descending sequence and alternating colour, ending in the black Aces.

The play: This is exactly as in calculation (page 167), except that one redeal is allowed when the stock pile is exhausted.

Daphne du Maurier refers to Patience in her novel *The King's General*, a story of the Civil War. Her card knowledge was obviously less advanced than her writing ability – no Patience games existed at the time of the Civil War!

Tower of Hanoy

Another old form of patience, which is based purely on skill. If played correctly it will always work out. But how long it takes will depend very much on the player. My best is seven minutes – perhaps you can do better.

One advantage of Tower of Hanoy is the fact that it uses only nine cards, so that it can be played in a confined space, such as a train carriage, without inconveniencing others.

Cards: Select nine cards from one suit, the 2 to the 10 inclusive.

Setting out: Shuffle the cards thoroughly, then deal them in three rows of three.

Objective: To get all the cards into a single column, starting with the 10 and descending to the 2.

Rules: Only the bottom card from each column can be moved. It may be moved to the bottom of another column, but only below a card of a higher value.

When a column is completely cleared, the vacancy may be filled by moving the bottom card from one of the other two columns into the vacancy.

Example: Suppose the cards are dealt out as follows:

The first objective must be to bring 10H to the top of a column.
The following moves would achieve this:

1   Move 4H under 10H.
2   Move 6H under 7H.
3   Move 4H under 6H.
4   Move 3H under 4H.
5   Move 10H into column vacated by 3H.

The next objective would be to bring 9H under 10H. Try it!

The Demon

Patience is not generally considered to be a gambling game. However, the inventor of The Demon, Richard A. Canfield, was a very well-known nineteenth-century gambler, and having invented the game he was determined to make some money out of it. This he did by offering to sell a pack of cards to a prospective player for $52.00, under the agreement that he would pay them $5.00 for every card in the foundation row after The Demon had been played. It has been estimated that the mercenary Mr Canfield stood to make $20–$25 each time.

Despite, or perhaps because of the difficulty in concluding The Demon, it is still extremely popular – perhaps the most widely played single-pack Patience in the world.

Cards: One normal pack is used.

Setting out: Deal thirteen cards face down as a reserve. The top card of the reserve is now turned up. Four more cards are dealt face up to the right of the reserve, to form bases for packing. The next card is placed face up above the bases to form a foundation for building. The set-up will look something like this:

Foundation card

Reserve

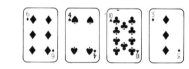

Packing bases

Objective: To build four round-the-corner suit sequences on the foundation cards (the three cards of the same rank as the first foundation card being placed alongside it when they appear).

The play: Cards are played either on to the foundation cards in ascending sequence, or on to the packing bases in descending alternate-colour sequence. Where possible the top card of the reserve is played and the next turned over. Alternatively, the stock is turned up, three cards at a time.

At any time the bottom card of a packing column can be played on to a foundation. Sequences can be moved from one column to another, but only as a complete unit.

Where a space occurs among the columns, it must be filled immediately with the top card from the reserve. If the reserve is exhausted, the space must be filled from the top of the upturned stock – but this can be delayed until an appropriate card appears.

The stock can be dealt and redealt, and the game ends either in success, or when no further move is possible.

Strategy: Try to clear the reserve as quickly as possible, and think before building on the foundations – it may be best to leave some cards available for packing.

Spaces

This is an 'open' form of Patience, where all the cards are exposed. It is also one where skill plays an important role. It is not always possible to reach a successful conclusion, but good play can increase the odds considerably.

Cards: One normal pack is used.

Setting out: Deal all fifty-two cards, in four rows of thirteen. Remove the four Aces, to leave four spaces.

Objective: To engineer the cards so that each row contains one suit only, descending from the King on the left to the 2 on the right.

The play: Each space must be filled with the next card down from the card to the left of the space. For example, if a row reads:

 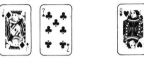

two possible moves would be 8S into the space following 9S, or 6C into the space following 7C. Obviously if 8S were moved, this would create a space following 10D in the above example.

Where spaces occur following 2s, no card can be moved. When there are four such spaces, the cards which are not correctly ordered (i.e. with Kings at the left of the rows, and descending in sequence) are gathered up, shuffled, and redealt, after reinserting the Aces. Two redeals are allowed. If the cards have not come out at this stage, the game has been lost.

Strategy: The order of the moves can have a major bearing on the course of the game. It is best to avoid creating spaces following 2s. This can sometimes be done by creating a space after the appropriate 3, so that the dangerous 2 can be moved out of harm's way.

When played well, it is estimated that the odds on a successful conclusion are in favour rather than against. So if you cannot get this Patience to come out, perhaps you need to think a bit harder!

171

Klondike

When I was first introduced to Patience, this was the game I learnt to play. I was by no means unique; to many people this is Patience. Along with The Demon, it is the most widely played form of the game.

Cards: One normal pack is used.

Setting out: Deal out twenty-eight cards, in seven overlapping rows. The first row should contain seven cards, the second row six, the third five and so on. The top card of each column should be turned up. The set-up will look something like this:

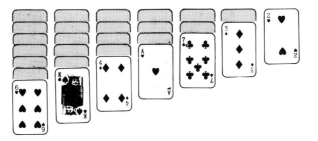

Objective: To build four ascending suit sequences, using the Aces as foundations, and ending up with the Kings.

The play: The Aces should be removed when they appear, and placed above the columns to form building foundations. Other cards can be moved on to the foundations, or packed on the seven columns in descending alternate colour sequence. When the top face-up card of a column is moved, the face-down card above it is turned over. The same applies if a sequence is moved from one column to another. If a column is cleared, it can be filled, but only by a King. When no further moves can be made, cards are turned up from the stock pile, one at a time.

Whether a card is built on to the foundations or retained on the packing columns is at the discretion of the player.

If the stock pile is exhausted and no further moves are possible, the game is lost.

Example: In the above layout, the following moves are possible:

1 Move AH to set up a foundation.
2 Move 2H on to AH.
3 Move KS into space vacated by 2H.
4 Move 6H on to 7C.

The face-down cards exposed by these moves can now be turned up, so further moves may be possible. If not, it is time to start on the stock pile.

King Albert
My personal favourite of the single-pack Patiences. It combines skill and luck in just the right proportions; it works out often enough to retain the interest, but not so often that the pleasure of success if diminished. In a word, it is compulsive!

Cards: One normal pack is used.

Setting out: Deal out forty-five cards, face-up, in nine overlapping rows. The first row should have nine cards, the second eight, the third seven and so on. The remaining seven cards form a reserve which is also open to the player. The set-up will look something like this:

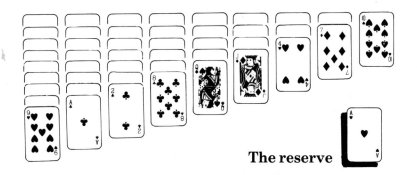

The reserve

173

Objective: To build four ascending suit sequences, using the Aces as foundations, and ending up with the Kings.

The play: The Aces should be removed to form building foundations as and when they appear. The seven cards in the reserve and the bottom cards on the columns are available for play. Cards can be moved either on to the foundations, or packed on the columns in descending alternate-colour sequence. Only one card can be moved at a time – sequences are *not* transferable from column to column.

When a column is cleared, any playable card can be moved into the vacancy.

Cards can be moved back from the top of the foundations on to the packing columns if this is beneficial.

The game ends either in success, or when no further moves are possible.

Strategy: The four Aces should be freed up and made available for building as early as possible. The most important aspect of strategy involves column vacancies. They should not necessarily be filled immediately, because they form the only means by which whole sequences can be moved. For example, consider that you have a two-card sequence 9H, 8S, and you wish to move it to the 10C which is available for packing. Because 9H is not exposed, it cannot be moved; however, if a vacant column exists, 8S can be moved into the vacancy, 9H can be moved on to 10C, then 8S can be moved on to 9H, thus retaining the vacancy. More vacant columns allow more cards to be moved in this way; two columns for four cards, three columns for eight cards and so on.

Care should also be taken over the order of play. In the sample layout above, moving 10S on to JD will give a vacancy. However, if 9H had already been moved on to 10S, this would no longer be possible.

Clock

Whilst not being one of the more skilful or exciting members of the Patience family, this is certainly one of the prettiest.

Cards: One normal pack is used.

Setting out: Deal, face down, forty-eight cards in twelve piles of four, set out so as to correspond to the face of a clock.

Objective: To have, face up, the four Aces in the one o'clock position, the four 2s at two o'clock, and so on.

The play: Turn over the first of the four undealt cards. Place it, face up, under the four cards at the corresponding position on the clock face. The Jack is equivalent to eleven, and the Queen to twelve. Having placed the card, turn over the top one of the four in that position, then repeat the manoeuvre.

When a King is turned up, place it in the centre, and turn over the second of the undealt cards.

Following the appearance of the first King, the game might look something like this:

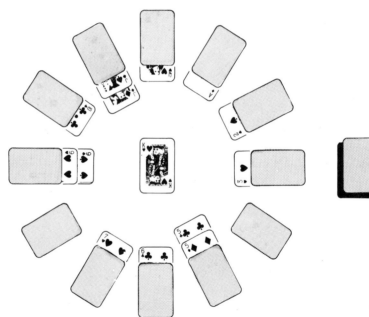

Under normal circumstances the game would not come out unless the fourth King was the last card to be turned up. So one 'chance' is allowed; if the fourth King appears before the end, it can be placed at the bottom of one of the twelve piles, face down, with the top card in the pile being turned over to continue with the game.

174

Flower Garden

Alternatively known as **Bouquet**, this is another pretty Patience, but this time with the emphasis on skill rather than luck.

Cards: One normal pack is used.

Setting out: Deal, face up, six columns of six overlapping cards. These are the *beds*. The remaining sixteen cards should be spread out in the player's hand. This is the *bouquet*. The set-up should look something like this:

Beds

Bouquet

Objective: To build four ascending suit sequences, using the Aces as bases, and building up to the Kings.

The play: Cards can either be built on the bases, or packed on the beds, in descending sequence, regardless of suit. Any card from the bouquet can be played at any time. Initially, only the bottom card of a bed can be played, although as the game progresses complete sequences can be moved from one bed to another.

When a column is cleared, it can be filled either with a card from the bouquet, or with a sequence or card from one of the beds.

The game ends when the objective is achieved, or when no further play is possible.

Strategy: The first priority is to free the four Aces. In the above layout, the Ace of hearts is immediately available from the bouquet, whereas the other three Aces must be released from their respective columns through judicious movements of the cards.

If possible, avoid using the cards from the bouquet whilst freeing other cards. They may be required later on. In general, good play results in a success rate greater than fifty per cent.

Double-Pack Patience Games

The emphasis in double-pack Patience games switches from the luck of the cards to the skill of the player.

These are games for the connoisseur rather than the dabbler.

It is probably worth investing in two packs of specialist Patience playing cards, which are smaller and more manouevrable than normal cards, before embarking on these games.

Miss Milligan

This is one of the oldest double-pack Patience games, although its origins and the source of its name are unknown. Perhaps Miss Milligan was a character similar to the little old lady created by the novelist E. F. Benson, who always manages to arrange for her Patience game to come out successfully just as her servants call her for Evening Prayers.

Cards: Two normal packs are used.

Objective: To build eight ascending suit-sequences, starting with the Aces and building to the Kings.

The play: Deal out eight cards in a row face-up. Any Aces should be removed to form foundations. Other cards are packed, where possible, in descending alternate-colour sequences.

When no further moves are possible, a further eight cards are dealt, overlapping existing cards or filling spaces. Aces are removed as foundations whenever they appear. Where possible, cards are built on to foundations, otherwise they are packed as before, with full or partial sequences being transferrable from column to column.

If a column is cleared, the vacancy can only be filled by a King, or sequence headed by a King.

Each time a stalemate occurs, with no further moves possible, eight more cards are dealt.

Once the stock is exhausted, the player is given an additional chance in the form of *waiving*. This allows the player to remove an exposed card, holding it in reserve while further building and packing takes place, until the removed card can be replaced correctly in the layout. If it cannot, the game has been lost. Only one card can be waived at a time, but the process can be repeated indefinitely providing the card-replacement rule is observed.

Strategy: The major skill element lies in the movements of sequences and partial sequences from column to column. It is therefore best to avoid blocking a sequence. The most dangerous cards from this point of view are the Kings – try to clear vacancies so as to get the Kings to the top of the columns.

The chance of success at Miss Milligan is not high; it has been estimated to be approximately one in twenty.

176

Giant

This is a variation on Miss Milligan where the success rate is considerably higher.

The game is played in exactly the same way, except that there are two important concessions to the player:

1. Vacant columns need not be filled by Kings. Instead they can be filled by any card.
2. Cards can be moved back from the foundations on to the packing columns.

These two small changes actually tip the odds in favour of the player.

In 1907, the New York financial world was in turmoil. Much depended on the actions of wealthy financier J. P. Morgan. While Wall Street waited, he played Patience, the famous old game of Miss Milligan. Finally he came to his decision; he cleared away the cards, put his support into the stock market, and waited while the panic slowly subsided.

177

Sultan

This is a fairly simple game, but one with a particularly pleasing end position when it is successful.

Cards: Two normal packs are used.

Setting out: Remove the eight Kings and one of the heart Aces from the pack. They should be arranged in a 3 × 3 square with the Ace of hearts in the middle of the top row, and with one of the heart Kings in the centre. The other seven Kings can be placed anywhere. Now deal four cards in two columns on either side of the square. The set-up will look something like this:

Objective: To build eight ascending suit sequences, topped by the eight Queens. The King of hearts is not built on. At the end of the game he is the 'Sultan' surrounded by his harem of Queens.

The play: The four cards on either side of the central square are available for building, as is the top card of the stock pile, which is turned up one card at a time. Unplayable cards are put on a waste heap, the top card of which is also available for building.

Aces are built on to Kings, so in the above diagram the Ace of diamonds can be played on to one of the diamond Kings, and the 2 of hearts on to the heart Ace.

Vacancies in the columns of playable cards are filled either from stock or from the top of the waste heap. They need not be filled immediately.

When the stock pile is exhausted, the waste heap is shuffled and redealt. Two such redeals are permitted.

Strategy: The skill in Sultan lies in the management of the vacancies. It is usually best to leave a vacancy until a card appears which is likely to be required shortly for building purposes.

The Windmill

The Windmill is a slightly unorthodox building game which derives its name from the pretty pictorial form of the layout.

Cards: Two normal packs are used.

Setting out: Remove any Ace from the pack and place it on the table, then deal two cards above and below it, and two cards to either side. These form the sails of the windmill. If a King has appeared, remove it and place it between two of the windmill's sails; deal another card from stock to replace it. The layout at this point may look something like this:

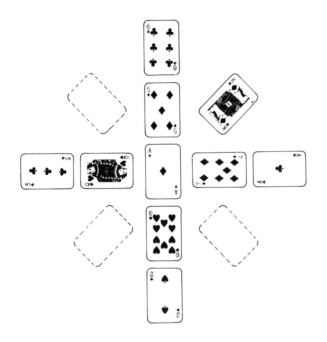

Objective: To build four descending sequences on the first four Kings to appear, ending with the Aces, and to build a fifty-two card suite on the central Ace, from Ace through King four times. All sequences are regardless of colour or suit.

The play: As in *Sultan*, the eight non-base cards, the top card in stock and the top card of the waste heap are available for building.

The first four Kings to appear are placed as in the diagram above.

In the diagram 2S and 3C can be built on to AH, and QH can be built on to KD.

When holes appear in the windmill's sails, they can be filled either from the stock pile or from the top of the waste heap. It is not necessary to mend a hole immediately!

The stock pile is turned up one card at a time.

There is no redeal, although if the game has not worked out when the stock is exhausted, the waste heap can be turned over and played one card at a time. This may result in vacancies occurring, in which case the game can carry on.

Strategy: As in *Sultan*, the art lies in the management of the vacancies, and which cards should be used to fill them.

A version of The Windmill can be played with one pack, although it is a less challenging game.

In One-deck Windmill the four Aces are placed in a square, where they take no further part in the game, and two cards are dealt out above and below and to either side to form the sails.

As the 2s appear they are placed between the sails and are built in sequence to the Kings. Suit and colour are unimportant.

Rules are exactly the same as for the two-pack version, but no central suite is formed.

To cheat oneself at Patience is the hallmark of the lowest form of human life.

The British Blockade

There is no military aspect to this game. *Blockade* refers to an element of the game; *British* distinguishes it from an inferior French version. Nevertheless, it is a game where strategic planning and regimental precision are needed to produce a favourable outcome.

Cards: Two normal packs are used.

Setting out: Remove an Ace and a King from each suit, and place them in two columns at either side of the playing area. Deal ten cards in a row between the top Ace and King. The layout will look something like this:

Objective: To build four ascending suit-sequences on the Aces, ending in the Kings, and four descending suit-sequences on the Kings, ending in the Aces.

The play: Any cards in the top row are available for building. In the example, 2C can be played on AC, and QH and JH on KH. Spaces thus created are filled from stock. When no further moves are possible a second row of ten cards is dealt below the first.

Further building and filling take place until a situation is reached when no card can be played from either row. At this point a third row of ten cards is dealt. This causes the middle row to become unplayable. The cards in it are *blockaded*. Only when the card above or below is removed does a card in the middle row become available. In short, only cards with their top or bottom exposed can be played.

It might seem that the game is virtually automatic, with the order of the cards being critical. However, the player does have scope for a certain degree of control as a consequence of the following two rules:

1   The top card of stock can be looked at before each move.
2   It is not necessary to carry out all possible building before refilling the rows, although when refilling does take place *every* vacancy must be filled, starting at the top and moving left to right along each row.

If convenient, cards can be moved from Ace suites to King suites, and vice versa. For example, if 6H is available for building, the ascending suite is topped by 7H (waiting for 8H) and the descending suite is topped by 8H (waiting for 7H), 7H can be transferred from one suite to the other so that 6H can be built on to it.

When the stock is exhausted, if the game has not worked out one concession is allowed. A buildable card can be removed from a blocked position, freeing in turn the cards on either side of it. If the game still fails to come out, it has been lost.

Strategy: Through knowing the top card of stock, a decision can be made as to whether it is likely to be needed soon. If so, it is often wise to build a card from the top row, so that the known card is inserted in a position where it will become readily available. Conversely, if the top stock card is unlikely to be required early, avoid playing a card from the top row, as the stock card may well block others below it.

The most interesting stage of the game often involves the late concession to the player. What might look like a totally intractable layout can miraculously change if the right blockage is cleared.

Patience is the art of hoping.

(Vauvenargues – *Reflections and Maxims* 1746)

Tolstoy was an inveterate Patience player.

The Emperor

This is one of several Patience games reputedly invented and played by the Emperor Napoleon during his exile on St Helena. However, despite the many free hours at his disposal, modern research indicates that Napoleon never actually played Patience. Rather it was his aide Las Cases, instructed by the Emperor to 'make the cards run more smoothly', who embarked on Patience games to achieve this objective.

A well-documented account of this incident reveals Napoleon to be a man whose temperament would not have been ideally suited to Patience. Following a mistake by the Emperor while attempting to deal, it was said of him: 'I could not have conceived that so trifling an accident could have affected any human creature so seriously – his whole countenance was lighted up with fury, and he made a violent contortion of his features, and drew down his mouth on one side, like one suffering an inward pang.'

Cards: Two normal packs are used.

Setting out: Deal out three rows of ten cards, face down. These form ten *sealed packets*. Now deal ten cards face up below the sealed packets. The layout will look something like this:

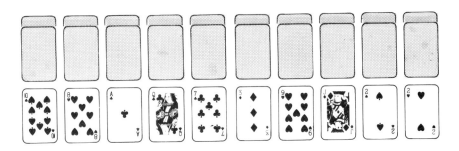

Objective: To build eight ascending suit-sequences on the Aces, leading up to the Kings.

The play: The Aces are removed whenever they appear, to form building foundations.

The sealed packets can only be opened when the cards below are removed (*breaking the seal*). Cards can be removed by being built on to foundations, or being packed, in columns, in descending alternate colour sequence.

In the above diagram, AC would immediately be removed as a foundation card, and the top card of the sealed packet above it would be turned up. This would now become available for building or packing. No replacement card is moved into the bottom row.

Only the bottom card in a column, the *exposed* card, is available for play. Thus in the diagram, if 10S is moved on to JD, then JD can no longer be moved on to QC. An exposed card can be moved from one column to another if it can be packed in sequence.

At any stage, regardless of whether further building or packing is possible, the stock pile can be turned up, one card at a time. Unplayable cards are placed face up in a waste heap. The top cards of the stock pile and the waste heap are always available for play, in addition to the bottom cards of the columns.

When a sealed packet is cleared totally, creating a vacant column, any playable card can be moved into the vacancy.

Where helpful, cards can be moved back from the building bases to the packing columns.

If the game has not worked out when the stock pile is exhausted, the waste heap is turned over and the top three cards removed for building or packing. Any card that is played can be replaced from the top of the waste heap. Only when all three cards are unplayable has the game been lost.

Strategy: It is often unwise to pack cards indiscriminately. The more cards that are packed below a sealed packet, the more cards have to be removed for the seal to be broken.

The main objectives must be to clear the sealed packets and, having cleared them, create vacancies which allow whole sequences to be moved, as in the single-pack game King Albert.

Don't be frightened of a big waste heap. A few vacant columns towards the end of the game can clear it miraculously.

Competitive Patience Games

Competitive Patience games come in three forms.

In the first type, everyone has identical cards, and the winner is the player who uses them most skilfully.

The second method involves each player playing the same game, but with different cards, the winner being the player who achieves the best result on the hand.

The third, and undoubtedly the most anarchic form of Patience, is the racing game, where the objective is simply to be first past the post. Requirements include expendable packs of cards, plenty of space, and preferably a sound-proofed room!

At least one example of each is included.

Crabbage
Definitely this is one for the old cards. Any completed suite is no longer required and, in the words of an eminent Patience authority, Mary Whitmore Jones, 'it is generally thrown on the floor, as this game allows no time for small ceremonies'.

Cards: One normal pack for each player.

Objective: To be the first to get rid of all one's cards.

The play: Everyone plays simultaneously, with each player holding his pack face down.

Whenever an Ace appears it forms a new building base. Suites are built from Aces to Kings, regardless of suit. Any player can build on to any suite. When a suite is completed, it is discarded.

Each player turns his cards, building if possible, or placing on a personal waste heap. When a player runs out of cards, he turns over the waste heap and starts again.

The first player to finish his pack is the winner.

Strategy: Be aggressive!

Racing Demon
Any one-person Patience game can be played competitively – Demon (see page 170) is probably the most popular version to be adapted in this way. Each player has a separate pack, distinguishable by the patterns or colours on the back of the cards. Then everyone plays a game of Demon. The only difference from the single-person game is that any player can build on to another's suit sequences. The winner is the first player to get rid of the thirteen cards in the reserve pile.

Golf

This game's name comes from the method of scoring. But be prepared for some fairly unprofessional totals!

Cards: One normal pack for each player.

Setting out: Deal out five rows of seven cards – these form the golf links. The remaining cards form a stock, the top card of which is turned up. The set-up will look like this:

The links

The receiving card

Objective: To clear as many cards from the links as possible.

The play: Cards are removed from the links and placed in the receiving pile (the *hole*) according to the following rules:

1   Only the bottom card from a column can be played.
2   The card played must be next in sequence, either up or down, to the top card on the receiving pile. Suit is unimportant.

When no further cards can be played, the next card from stock is turned on to the receiving pile, and the play repeated. This goes on until the stock is exhausted.

The number of cards remaining on the links represents the score for the hole. The player with the lowest score wins the hole.

When the links are cleared completely, any cards remaining in stock are deducted from zero to give a minus score on the hole. If no cards remain, the score is zero itself. This represents very good golf indeed. Conversely, I once registered twenty-three on a hole – the equivalent of being very badly bunkered!

Poker Patience

Poker Patience can also be played as a solitaire game, but is best in a competitive framework. Whether it is played for money is a personal decision.

Cards: One normal pack for each player.

Preliminary: One player is appointed *dictator*, preferably the player with the loudest voice and clearest diction, for it is his job to call out cards as they are turned up.

The play: Only the dictator need have a shuffled pack of cards, which is held face down. He turns the top card and calls it out. Each player selects that same card from his packs, placing it on the playing area in front of them. This includes the dictator.

He then turns the second card, similarly calling it out. It must be placed next to the first card, above, below, to either side or diagonally adjacent. For example, if the first card was 7C as below, the second card could be placed in any of the eight positions indicated:

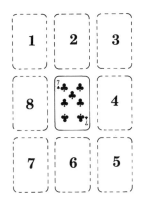

The dictator continues to call out cards, up to a total of twenty-five. Each must be placed next to at least one other card, and when the last one has been called the twenty-five cards must form a 5 × 5 square.

The objective in placing the cards is to form Poker hands, either across the rows or down the columns. Once a card has been placed, it cannot be moved. The scoring is as follows:

Straight flush (five cards in suit and sequence)	30 points
Four of a kind (four cards of the same rank)	16 points
Straight (five cards in sequence, any suit)	12 points
Full house (three of a kind + a pair)	10 points
Three of a kind (three cards of the same rank)	6 points
Flush (five cards of the same suit)	5 points
Two pairs	3 points
One pair	1 point

The Ace can count high or low in sequences, but these cannot go *round the corner*. In other words, A–2–3–4–5 and 10–J–Q–K–A are fine, but Q–K–A–2–3 is not.

The winner is the player scoring the most points.

To illustrate the scoring, I have just played out a Poker hand. The final situation was as follows:

HORIZONTAL			VERTICAL		
1	Straight	12	1	Three 10s	6
2	Pair of Jacks	1	2	Three 8s	6
3	Straight	12	3	Three 7s	6
4	Pair of 9s	1	4	–	0
5	Flush	5	5	–	0
	Total	31			18

Total Score: 31 + 18 = 49 points

Card Player's Jargon

Ascending sequence (*Patience*): Two or more adjacent cards, each one higher than the previous one.

Auction: The period of bidding.

Available card (*Patience*): Any card which can be played.

Bank/banker: The player who takes in the bets, usually the dealer in a gambling game; the casino.

Base (*Patience*): The card from which ascending sequences are built.

Bet: A wager on the outcome of a game.

Bid: A statement of intent to achieve a particular result in a hand; to make such a statement.

Bidder: A player making a bid.

Blocked (*Patience*): In a state such that no further moves are possible.

Bluff: An attempt to deceive in a gambling game.

Build (*Patience*): To move cards on to a base.

Call: To bid or pass; the act of doing so.

Cash: To play a winning card.

Chip: A unit of gambling currency.

Column (*Patience*): A descending line of cards.

Combination: Two or more cards which go together well for the purposes of the game being played.

Contract: The final statement of intent following a series of bids.

Court card: Any King, Queen or Jack.

Cover: To play a higher card of the same suit.

Dead card: Any card which takes no further part in the play.

Deadwood: Unmatched cards in a game of rummy.

Deal: To distribute the cards before play; the act of doing so.

Dealer: The player who deals.

Dealer's choice (*Poker*): The prerogative of the dealer to choose which version should be played.

Deck: A complete set of cards.

Declaration: A successful bid, which determines the final contract.

Declarer: The player who has made the declaration.

Defence: The opponents of the declarer.

Descending sequence: Two or more adjacent cards, each one lower than the previous one.

Discard: To throw a worthless card; the act of doing so.

Distribution: The way in which the cards are divided between the players.

Down: Having failed to fulfil a contract.

Draw: To take a card from a stock pile; to take a card from a complete deck, in order to determine which player is dealer, and which players are to partner each other.

Dummy: The player who takes no further part in the hand following a sequence of bids in bridge; his hand, which is controlled by the declarer.

Eligible card (*Patience*): Any card which may be played.

Established: Having become a winner during the course of play.

Exchange: To draw new cards in order to replace old ones.

Fan (*Patience*): A group of cards which have been spread out so that all are visible.

Flush: A group of cards of the same suit.

Fold (*Poker*): To drop out of the hand, therefore forfeiting one's bet.

Follow suit: To play a card of the suit led.

Foundation (*Patience*): The card from which ascending sequences are built.

Full house (*Poker*): Three cards of the same rank, together with a pair.

Game: The number of points required to win; a subdivision of a rubber.

Group: A set of three or more cards which combine to form a scoring combination.

Hand: The cards dealt to a player; the period between one deal and the next.

Holding: The contents of a player's hand.

Honours: High cards with special scoring values.

Information: The disclosure of a player's holding through his actions during the course of play.

Jackpot: A big pot in a gambling game.

Joker: An extra card which is added to the standard deck for certain games, generally as a wild card.

Kitty: The pot in a gambling game.

Knave: The American term for a Jack.

Laydown: A hand which is so strong that it cannot fail to win.

Lay off (*Rummy*): To add cards to other players' melds.

Layout (*Patience*): The cards which are dealt to the table to form the game's starting point.

Lead: To play the first card to a trick; the card thus played.

Leader: The player making the lead.

Limit: The maximum amount which can be bet on a hand.

Long suit: A suit in which more than the average number of cards are held.

Major suit: In Bridge, one of the two higher suits, i.e. spades or hearts.

Make: To fulfil a contract.

Marriage (*Bezique etc*): A King and Queen in the same suit.

Meld: A completed group of cards, three or more of the same rank, or three or more in sequence; to form a meld.

Minor suit: In Bridge, one of the two lower suits, i.e. clubs or diamonds.

Misdeal: To deal out the cards incorrectly; the result of doing so.

No trump: A contract in which there is no trump suit.

Null/nullo: A bid to make no tricks.

Off: Having failed to fulfil a contract.

Open: To make the first bid; to make the first lead.

Opening bid: The first bid.

Opening lead: The lead to the first trick.

Overcall: To make a higher bid than the previous one; the bid thus made.

Overtrump: To play a higher trump card.

Pack: A complete set of cards.

Pack (*Patience*): To move cards on to columns, according to the rules of the game.

Pair: Two cards of the same rank.

Partial sequence (*Patience*): Part of a sequence.

Partner: Another player with whom one combines in the play of a hand.

Partnership: Two players acting as partners.

Pass: To decline to make a bid.

Percentage: The takings of a gambling establishment.

Picture card: Any King, Queen or Jack.

Pip: Any one of the suit symbols printed on a card; for example, a 9 has nine pips.

Plain suit: Any suit which is not the trump suit.

Play: To take part in a hand; to take one's turn; to place a card on a trick; the actions of doing so.

Playable card: A card which may be played to a trick, according to the rules of the game.

Play from hand: To play a card held in one's own hand.

Player: A person taking part in a game.

Pot: The total number of bets riding on a hand.

Raise: To make a higher bet; the action of doing so.

Rank: The position of a card within a suit.

Redeal: To deal the cards a second or subsequent time, generally as the result of a misdeal.

Reserve (*Patience*): A part of the layout which is available for play.

Revoke: Fail to follow suit, when obliged to do so; the act of revoking.

Round: A division of play in which all players have had the opportunity to take part.

Round-the-corner: Of a sequence, going from the highest card to the lowest card, e.g. K, A, 2.

Row (*Patience*): A horizontal line of cards.

Rubber: The winning score in certain games, which is achieved through the successful play of several hands.

Ruff: To win a trick by playing a trump card when a plain suit has been led; the act of doing so.

Run: A sequence of three or more cards of the same suit.

Sacrifice: To accept a small penalty in exchange for stopping one's opponents making a much larger score.

Sequence: Two or more cards of adjacent rank.

Set-up (*Patience*): The initial layout.

Shoe: A device used for dealing cards in certain gambling games.

Short suit: A suit in which less than the average number of cards are held.

Show: To expose one's hand; the act of doing so.

Shuffle: To mix the cards randomly, prior to the deal.

Side suit: Any suit which is not the trump suit.

Signal: To play a particular card in order to convey information; the act of doing so.

Slam: Twelve or thirteen tricks.

Stand: To accept the cards currently held, with no further need for exchange.

Stock (pile): The portion of the pack which has not been dealt, but which is available for drawing cards at a later stage.

Straight: A sequence of cards, not necessarily of the same suit.

Strip out: To remove certain cards from the pack, before the deal.

Suit: Any of the four sets of thirteen cards in a standard pack: spades, hearts, diamonds or clubs.

Suit sequence: A sequence in which all cards are of the same suit.

Tableau (*Patience*): The initial layout.

Tarot cards: A pack of cards now used primarily for divination purposes.

Touching: Of adjacent rank.

Trick: A round of cards during the play.

Trump: A privileged card which, for the duration of the hand, ranks higher than any card of a plain suit.

Trump suit: A suit comprising trump cards.

Undertricks: The number of tricks by which a contract has failed to be fulfilled.

Unload: To throw a worthless card.

Unplayable: A card which cannot be played to a trick, according to the rules of the game.

Upcard: A card turned up from the stock pile.

Vacancy (*Patience*): The space where a column has been totally cleared.

Variation/Variant: A new version of a standard game.

Void: A suit in which no cards are held.

Waste heap: A pile of discarded cards.

Widow: An extra hand which may or may not take a further part in the play.

Wild card: A card which can be made to represent another card of any suit or rank.

Winner: A card which wins, or is destined to win, a trick.